2,001
Most Useful
FRENCH
Words

Heather McCoy, Ph.D.

DOVER PUBLICATIONS, INC.
Mineola, New York

Copyright

Copyright © 2010 by Heather McCoy
All rights reserved.

Bibliographical Note

2,001 Most Useful French Words is a new work, first published by
Dover Publications, Inc., in 2010.

Library of Congress Cataloging-in-Publication Data

McCoy, Heather.
   2,001 most useful French words / Heather McCoy.
      p. cm. — (Dover language guides)
   Includes bibliographical references.
   ISBN-13: 978-0-486-47615-5
   ISBN-10: 0-486-47615-4
   1. French language—Vocabulary.   2. French language—Usage.   3. French language—Grammar.   I. Title.   II. Title: Two thousand and one most useful French words.
   PC2445M33 2010
   448.2'421—dc22   2010034730

Manufactured in the United States by Courier Corporation
47615401
www.doverpublications.com

Contents

Acknowledgments

I would like to thank those who have assisted me with this project, directly and indirectly. I gratefully acknowledge Rochelle Kronzek and Janet Kopito, editors at Dover Publications, for the opportunity to create a book that allowed me to immerse myself in the glory of words; Sandrine Siméon, for her careful proofreading and helpful suggestions; Bénédicte Monicat, for being a stellar colleague; the students at Penn State University, who continue to teach me so much; and my husband, Gary J. Weisel, whose sense of dedication to hard work will always be a source of inspiration to me.

Introduction

This book is intended for anyone who wishes to enrich his or her French vocabulary. Readers will find a review of well-known terms, as well as many new and useful words. The structure of the book permits it to be used in a variety of ways, either alphabetically for a systematic review, or randomly, to dip in for a casual perusal. This flexibility will contribute to the book's usefulness.

The first section of the book contains an alphabetical listing of all 2,001 words. Each word is listed in French, with the English translation immediately following. The gender of nouns is indicated as masculine (m.) or feminine (f.); plural nouns are indicated as well (pl.). Adjectives are provided in the masculine form with the feminine form indicated in parentheses. In addition, each word is presented in a French sentence for context, followed by the English translation.

The second part of the book contains a Categories section. Here you will find simple vocabulary reference lists of common words that will be useful to you when you want to describe yourself, talk about your family, communicate while traveling, and many other purposes. These are terms that you have likely learned before—most of them are straightforward enough that contextual information isn't provided. The Categories section also includes a useful Vocabulary Tips section that provides insight about how you can use English to figure out the meaning of French words, and vice versa. A *Faux Amis* guide lists words that seem to mean the same thing in both French and English, but, in fact, do not!

The last section of the book contains a short grammar review, complete with helpful charts containing verb conjugations, subject pronouns, and adjective formation. A short guide to prepositions, negation, and question formation is also provided.

A word about context: One of the most important tools we have for discerning meaning in language is context. This is true for our native language, as well as for languages we learn as non-native speakers. You might not know what the word "punctilious" means in English, but when you see the sentence "I can think of no better way to describe Margaret than "punctilious"—she shows the highest regard for correct behavior, and proper etiquette is always her primary concern," the meaning of "punctilious" will be clear. You can figure out from the context that "punctilious" likely means *socially correct* and *mindful of good manners and conventions*. A word can also mean very different things depending on the words around it. The sentences "This sweater is green" and "My cousin is interested in green technologies" use the word "green" in different ways, and it is the rest of the sentence that makes the intended meaning evident. In this book we are limited to contextual clues at the sentence level, but in the world beyond this book, contextual clues reach far beyond the sentence. Elements such as the age of the speaker(s), the person who is being addressed (and by whom), the place where these words are being uttered, and even whether humor is intended, all offer potential contextual clues for meaning. Keep this in mind when you hear the words in this book being used in new or unexpected ways.

We believe that *2,001 Most Useful French Words* will provide an eminently useful tool, however you choose to use it. Our goal is for this handy book to be an indispensable tool in your further explorations in the French language. Immerse yourself in the pleasure of the words as you read it. *Bonne lecture!*

French Pronunciation Guide

Here are some general principles of pronunciation:

Nasalization

In French, a vowel is nasalized when it is followed by a single *m* or *n* in the same syllable. The transcription of these nasalized vowels appears as:

-an, -am, -em, -en -> ahn, ehn
-in, -im -> ihn, ihm
-on, -om -> ohn, ohm
-um, -un -> uhn

To produce a nasalized vowel, quickly pass the air through both the nose and the mouth at the same time. The *m* or *n* isn't pronounced after the nasal vowel, as follows:

français -> frahn-say ; *temps* -> tahn
pain -> pihn ; *printemps* ->prihn-tehn
bon -> bohn
quelqu'un -> kell-kuhn

Silent Final Consonants

In French, most consonants at the end of a word are silent, although there are exceptions to this rule: *c*, *f*, and *l*. The consonant *r* also is pronounced, but is silent when occurring in the endings *-er* and *-ier*.

The French r

The French *r* can be one of the most challenging sounds for English speakers to pronounce. Pronunciation of the *r* will depend upon the region of the French-speaking world that you are visiting. In some areas, the French *r* can resemble the Italian or Spanish *r*—produced by rolling it on the tip of the tongue. The Parisian *r* is a more gutteral sound: it's helpful to imagine the sound being produced in the back of the throat, the same place that produces the *h* in "ahoy." The *r* is voiced, meaning that there is a slight vibration of the vocal chords.

The Plural s

As mentioned above, consonants at the end of words normally are not pronounced. Make special note of this when pronouncing the *s* that denotes the plural:

Le chat -> luh shah
Les chats -> lay shah

Notice how the pronunciation of the noun *chat* does not change between the singular and the plural. This is quite different from English, and is important for English speakers to remember.

Liaison

A final consonant that is normally silent is pronounced when it comes before a vowel or *h*. This phenomenon is called *liaison*. Note the following change:

A final *s* before a consonant: *des livres* -> day leev-ruh
A final *s* before a vowel: *des animaux* -> daze ehn-ee-moh

The rules for liaison can be somewhat complex, so simply pay attention to the phonetic transcriptions in order to get a feel for when its usage is appropriate.

Stress

The last syllable of a French word is usually stressed:

Beaucoup -> boh-<u>koo</u>

However, when the last syllable is an unstressed *e* (*uh* in the transcription used here), the next-to-the-last syllable receives the stress:

Formidable -> for-mee-<u>dah</u>-bluh

You will also notice that in addition to the stress at the end of a word, there also is stress at the end of a phrase:

Je suis américain et travaille au musée d'art contemporain.-> zhuh swee <u>za</u>-mary-<u>kihn</u> ay tra-vy oh moo-<u>zay</u> <u>dar</u> cohn-<u>tehn</u>-por-<u>ihn</u>.

Scheme of Pronunciation

Letters	Transcription	Example	Notes
a	a	as in *ask*, but cut short	
	ah	as in *father*	
ai	ay	as in *play*	
	y	as in *why*	
au	oh	as in *bow*	See note on *o* below.
b	b	as in *bear*	
c	k	as in *car*	Pronounced *k* before *a*, *o*, or *u*

	s	as in *sun*	Pronounced *s* before *e* and *i*
ç	s	as in *sun*	
d	d	as in *danger*	Formed by touching tongue tip to teeth
e, è	eh	as in *met*	
é	ay	as in *play*	
e, eu, œu	uh	as in *bubble*	
f	f	as in *fan*	
g	g	as in *give*	Before *a, o,* and *u*
g	zh	as in *garage*	Before *e* and *i*
gn	ny	as in *canyon*	
h	silent		
i	ee	as in *feet*	
j	zh	as in *garage*	
k	k	as in *kernel*	
l	l	as in *lap*	
m	m	as in *me*	
n	n	as in *note*	
o	oh	as in *toe*	
oi	wa	as in *want*	
ou	oo	as in *boom*	
p	p	as in *pat*	
ph	f	as in *fan*	
q	k	as in *kernel*	
r	r	as in *red*	See section above.

s	ss	as in *lass*	At the beginning of the word or when doubled
	z	as in *zap*	When between two vowels
	silent		At the end of a word, unless followed by a vowel. See section above.
t	t	as in *tip*	
th	t	as in *tip*	
u	oo	no English equivalent	Formed by saying "ee," moving lips into rounded position without moving tongue.
v	v	as in *vote*	
w	v, w	as in *vote, win*	
x	ks	as in *licks*	
y	ee	as in *greet*	
z	z	as in *zoo*	

Alphabetical Section

A

à   *in, at, to*
Je dois aller à la mairie pour récupérer des documents.
I need to go to the town hall to pick up some documents.

abeille f.   *bee*
Elle est allergique aux piqûres d'abeilles.
She is allergic to bee stings.

abîmer   *ruin, damage, spoil*
Si tu ne fais pas attention, tu vas abîmer ton pantalon.
If you're not careful, you'll ruin your pants.

abonner, s'   *to subscribe*
Je veux m'abonner à cette revue, mais elle est trop chère.
I want to subscribe to this journal, but it's too expensive.

aborder   *to tackle, to approach*
On va faire attention en abordant ce problème.
We're going to be very careful when tackling this problem.

abri m.   *shelter*
Il y a un abri antiatomique chez mes grand-parents.
There's a bomb shelter at my grandparents' house.

absent(e)   *absent*
Il est souvent absent de notre classe.
He's frequently absent from our class.

absolument   *absolutely*
Il faut absolument que tu m'appelles demain.
You absolutely must call me tomorrow.

accablant(e)   *oppressive, damning*
Cette chaleur est vraiment accablante.
This heat is truly oppressive.

accepter   *to accept*
Le gouvernement accepte la responsabilité des problèmes
   du pays.
The government accepts responsibility for the country's problems.

accès m.   *access*
L'accès aux quais est interdit.
Access to the platforms is forbidden.

accompagner   *to accompany, go with*
Je peux vous accompagner?
May I accompany you?

accord m.   *accord, agreement*
Est-ce qu'il a donné son accord pour le projet?
Did he give his agreement for the project?

accro   *addict*
Elle passe des heures et des heures sur Facebook—c'est une accro!
She spends hours and hours on Facebook—she's an addict!

achat m.   *purchase*
Je sais que ce sac est un achat impulsif mais, je l'adore!
I know this handbag was an impulse purchase, but I love it!

acheter   *to buy*
Elle veut acheter cette voiture, mais elle n'a pas assez d'argent.
She wants to buy this car but doesn't have enough money.

action f.   *action.*
Mon cousin aime bien les films d'action.
My cousin loves action films.

actions f.   *stock or shares*
Comme il a des problèmes d'argent en ce moment, il doit vendre
   toutes ses actions.
Since he is having money problems, he needs to sell all his stocks.

actualité f.   *current events, news*
Ce problème fait toujours la une de l'actualité.
This problem is always in the headlines.

actuel(le)   *present, current*
Quel est l'état actuel de la situation politique dans votre pays?
*What is the current state of the political situation in your
   country?*

actuellement   *currently, at the time being*
On a peu de travail actuellement.
We have little work at the time being.

adapter   *to adapt*
Le cinéaste désire adapter cette pièce au cinéma.
The filmmaker wants to adapt this play for film.

adapter, s'   *to adjust to*
Tu dois t'adapter à la nouvelle situation.
You should adapt to the new situation.

addition f.   *bill, check*
L'addition, s'il vous plaît!
The check, please!

ado   *adolescent, teen*
Il est vrai que les films de vampires sont très appréciés par les
ados en ce moment.
It is true that vampire movies are really liked by teens these days.

adopter   *to adopt*
L'Assemblé nationale a décidé d'adopter cette nouvelle loi.
The National Assembly decided to adopt this new law.

adorer   *to adore*
Il adore les langues; il veut devenir prof de langues.
He loves languages; he wants to be a language teacher.

adresse f.   *address*
Quelle est votre adresse?
What's your address?

aéroport m.   *airport*
Ma navette part pour l'aéroport dans trois quarts d'heure.
My shuttle leaves for the airport in forty-five minutes.

affaiblir   *to weaken*
Cette infection affaiblit le jeune homme à tel point qu'il doit aller
aux urgences.
*This infection is weakening the young man to the point that he has to go
to the emergency room.*

affaire f.   *affair, matter*
Sois prudent, c'est une affaire louche.
Be careful, it's a shady deal.

affaires m. pl.   *business, business dealings*
Mon oncle est expert en affaires internationales.
My uncle is an expert in international business.

affamé(e)   *starving*
Ces réfugiés sont affamés.
These refugees are starving.

affectueux(-euse)   *affectionate*
Elle est toujours très affectueuse avec ses enfants.
She's always very affectionate with her children.

affliger   *to afflict, to distress*
Cette nouvelle les afflige.
This news is distressing to them.

affoler, s'   *to become panicked*
Ne t'affole pas, on va régler la situation.
Don't panic, we're going to fix the situation.

afin de / afin que   *in order to / so that*
Marc a pris un taxi afin d'arriver à l'heure à son rendez-vous.
Marc took a taxi in order to arrive at his appointment on time.
Il faut que tu étudies afin que je puisse emprunter ton manuel.
You have to study so that I can borrow your textbook.

agacer   *to annoy, to irritate*
Ces petits problèmes m'agacent beaucoup.
These little problems really annoy me.

âge m.   *age*
Elle a quel âge?
How old is she?

âgé(e)   *aged*
Cette dame âgée a survécu à toute sa famille, elle a presque cent ans.
*This elderly woman has survived all her family; she is almost one
    hundred years old.*

agence de voyages f.   *travel agency*
Je dois passer par l'agence de voyages afin d'acheter mon billet
    de train.
I need to stop by the travel agency to buy my train ticket.

agent *(de police)* m.   *police officer.*
Il y a un agent de police à l'appareil qui veut te parler!
There's a police office on the phone who wants to talk to you!

agréable   *agreeable, pleasant*
On a passé un après-midi agréable au jardin botanique.
We spent a pleasant afternoon at the botanical garden.

agriculteur m.   *farmer*
Mon oncle est agriculteur dans le Morvan.
My uncle is a farmer in the Morvan region.

aide f.   *help, assistance*
La majorité des fumeurs arrêtent sans aide.
The majority of smokers stop without assistance.

aider   *to help*
Je peux vous aider?
May I help you?

aigre   *sour*
Cette sauce est un peu trop aigre à mon avis.
This sauce is a little too sour, in my opinion.

aiguille f.   *needle*
Il me faut une aiguille à coudre.
I need a sewing needle.

ailleurs; d'ailleurs   *elsewhere; besides, moreover*
Si tu veux boire, il faut aller ailleurs.
If you want to drink, you'll have to go elsewhere.
On n'a pas réussi à l'examen, et d'ailleurs je dois admettre qu'on
    n'a même pas étudié!
*We didn't pass the test, and moreover, I must admit that we didn't even
    study!*

aimable   *nice, pleasant*
Notre nouveau collègue est assez aimable, en fait.
Our new colleague is, in fact, pretty nice.

aimer   *to love;*   **aimer bien**   *to like*
J'aime bien le jazz. Et toi?
I like jazz. And you?

aîné(e)   *elder*
Ma sœur aînée m'agace beaucoup.
My elder sister irritates me a lot.

ainsi   *like that, this way*
Si tu me parles ainsi, je te raccroche au nez!
If you talk to me like that, I'll hang up on you!

air m.   *air*
   On va à l'exterieur pour prendre de l'air.
   We're going outside to get some fresh air.

aire de jeu f.   *playground*
   Il y avait trop de monde cet après-midi sur notre aire de jeu
      préférée.
   *There were too many people this afternoon at our favorite
      playground.*

ajouter   *to add*
   Je n'ai rien à ajouter à cette discussion.
   I don't have anything to add to this discussion.

alambiqué(e)   *convoluted, obscure*
   Ses explications sont toujours alambiquées.
   His explanations are always too convoluted.

aléas m. pl   *uncertainties*
   Il y a trop d'aléas associés à ce projet.
   There are too many uncertainties associated with this project.

aller   *to go*
   Tu n'as pas envie d'y aller?
   You don't feel like going there?

allumer   *to light, to turn on, to ignite*
   Peux-tu allumer le gaz?
   Can you turn on the gas?

allumettes pl   *matches*
   Achète-moi des allumettes. Je n'en ai plus.
   Buy me some matches. I don't have any left.

alors   *so, then, therefore*
   Alors, ça s'est bien passé?
   So, did it go well?

améliorer   *to improve*
   Ils devraient améliorer leur produit avant de le vendre.
   They should improve their product before selling it.

amende f.   *fine*
   Si tu laisses ton chien libre dans le parc, tu recevras certainement
      une amende!
   If you let your dog loose in the park, you'll certainly receive a fine!

ami(e) m. (f.)   *friend*
Ça fait longtemps qu'on n'a pas vu notre ami Pierre.
We haven't seen our friend Peter for a long time.

amical(e)   *friendly*
On a eu une conversation assez amicale hier, mais aujourd'hui il
   refuse de me parler.
*We had a friendly enough conversation yesterday, but today he refuses
   to talk to me.*

amitié f.   *friendship*
L'amitié est très importante pour les adolescents.
Friendship is very important to adolescents.

amitiés, faire ses...à   *to give one's regards to*
Fais mes amitiés à ta famille.
Give my regards to your family.

ampoule f.   *light bulb*
Cette lampe a besoin d'une ampoule.
This lamp needs a light bulb.

amour m.   *love*
La conception de l'amour dans cette culture est très différente de
   la nôtre.
The concept of love in this culture is very different from ours.

amoureux(-euse)   *in love*
Il est amoureux d'elle.
He's in love with her.

ampleur f.   *size, scope*
Un problème de cette ampleur doit être pris en considération
   avant de procéder.
*A problem of this scope should be taken into consideration before
   proceeding.*

amuser, s'   *to have a good time, to enjoy oneself*
On s'est vraiment amusé chez nos voisins hier soir.
We had a really good time at our neighbors' house last night.

an m.   *year*
On a vu notre grand-père il y a trois ans à Angers.
We saw our grandfather three years ago in Angers.

anéantir   *to ruin, to crush, to shatter*
Cette pluie diluvienne inattendue risque d'anéantir nos récoltes cette année.
This unexpected torrential rain might ruin our crops this years.

anglais m.   *English*
Tu parles bien l'anglais.
You speak English well.

anglais(e)   *English*
Je viens de voir un film anglais qui m'a beaucoup impressionné.
I've just seen an English film that really impressed me.

Angleterre f.   *England*
J'ai très envie de visiter l'Angleterre l'été prochain.
I'm really eager to visit England next summer.

anicroche f.   *hitch*
Tout s'est déroulé sans anicroche.
Everything went off without a hitch.

animé(e)   *lively, animated*
On peut toujours compter sur Monique pour avoir un repas animé chez elle.
We can always count on Monique to have a lively meal at her place.

animer   *to get excited, to liven up, to lead*
Le présentateur a animé une discussion vive dans laquelle on a tous participé.
The speaker led a lively discussion in which we all participated.

anniversaire m.   *birthday*
Elle m'a donné un pull pour mon anniversaire.
She gave me a sweater for my birthday.

annonce f.   *notice, advertisement*
Si vous voulez changer votre nom, il faut l'indiquer dans une annonce dans le journal.
If you want to change your name, you have to put it in a notice in the newspaper.

annoncer   *to announce, to make known*
Est-ce qu'ils ont annoncé publiquement le nom du gagnant du prix?
Have they publicly announced the name of the prizewinner?

apaiser   *to calm, to appease*
Elle essaie d'appaiser son fils avant qu'il ne se fâche.
She's trying to calm her son down before he gets angry.

apiculture f.   *beekeeping*
L'apiculture est devenue très à la mode en ce moment.
Beekeeping has become very fashionable recently.

appareil m.   *appliance, camera*
Elle veut prendre des photos avec son nouvel appareil photo.
She wants to take pictures with her new camera.

appartement, appart (colloq.) m.   *apartment*
Tu devrais voir le nouvel appart de Jean-Marie, c'est incroyable!
You should see Jean-Marie's new apartment, it's incredible!

appartenir   *to belong*
Ce sac n'appartient à personne.
This bag doesn't belong to anyone.

appel m.   *appeal*
L'avocat fera un appel demain.
The lawyer will make an appeal tomorrow.

appeler   *to call*
Il va nous appeler avec les directions.
He's going to call us with the directions.

appeler, s'   *to be named*
Je m'appelle François, et vous?
I'm named Frank. And you?

apporter   *to bring*
Tu devrais apporter ton écran-solaire sur la plage.
You should bring your sunblock to the beach.

apprendre   *to learn*
On apprend à faire du snowboard.
We're learning to snowboard.

apprêter   *to prepare, to dispose someone to something*
Elle apprête un repas pour nous.
She is preparing a meal for us.

approcher, s'   *to approach, to draw closer*
Approche-toi pour que je te mouche le nez.
Come closer so I can wipe your nose.

appui m.   *support*
Ce candidat bénéficie de l'appui de nombreux syndicats.
This candidate is benefiting from the support of many unions.

après   *after*
Si on allait boire un coup après le film?
How about getting a drink after the movie?

après-midi m.   *afternoon*
Cet après-midi j'espère pouvoir lire le journal.
This afternoon I hope to be able to read the newspaper.

arbre m.   *tree*
Dans notre jardin il y a un arbre qui fleurit qui est absolument
    formidable.
There's a flowering tree in our garden that is absolutely marvelous.

architecte m., f.
Elle espère devenir architecte parce qu'elle s'intéresse aux
    technologies de construction verte.
*She hopes to become an architect because she's interested in "green"
    building technologies.*

argent m.   *money*
Tu peux me prêter de l'argent?
Can you lend me some money?

argent comptant, prendre pour   *to take at face value*
Ne prends pas ce qu'il dit pour argent compant.
Don't take what he says at face value.

arithmétique   *arithmetic*
Ma fille aime bien l'arithmétique.
My daughter really likes arithmetic.

armée f.   *army*
Il est soldat dans l'Armée américaine.
He's a soldier in the American army.

armoire f.   *wardrobe, linen cupboard*
Mets les serviettes dans cette armoire.
Put the towels in this cupboard.

arracher   *to pull up, to pull out, to snatch*
Je dois arracher toutes les mauvaises herbes du jardin.
I need to pull up all the weeds from the garden.

arranger   *to arrange, to fix*
Elle va arranger l'intérieur de son apartment pour mieux refléter ses goûts.
She's going to fix up her apartment so that it better reflects her tastes.

arrêt m.   *stop*
Est-ce qu'il y a un arrêt de bus près d'ici?
Is there a bus stop nearby?

arrêter   *to stop*
Si vous arrêtez de fumer, vous aurez plus d'argent de poche.
If you stop smoking you'll have more pocket money.

arrhes f. pl.   *deposit*
Vous devez verser des arrhes pour que le contrat soit conclu.
You need to pay a deposit so that the contract can be finalized.

arriere, en   *behind*
Il a fait un pas en arrière.
He took a step back.

arrière-goût m.   *aftertaste*
Ce fromage bleu a un arrière-goût assez désagréable.
This blue cheese has a somewhat disagreeable aftertaste.

arrière-pays m.   *hinterland*
Mon oncle vient d'un arrière-pays bien lointain.
My uncle comes from a remote hinterland.

arrière-pensée f.   *ulterior motive*
Si les gens me disent qu'ils m'aiment bien, je pense toujours qu'ils ont une arrière-pensée.
If people tell me they like me, I always think they have an ulterior motive.

arrivée f.   *arrival*
On attend avec impatience l'arrivée de la délégation chinoise.
We're impatiently awaiting the arrival of the Chinese delegation.

arriver   *to arrive*
Le train arrive à 10h45.
The train is arriving at 10:45 a.m.

arrogant(e)   *haughty, arrogant*
Il parle d'un air si arrogant que je ne fais plus attention à lui.
He speaks in such an arrogant way that I no longer pay attention to him.

arroser   *to water, to spray*
N'oubliez pas d'arroser mes plantes!
Don't forget to water my plants!

art m.   *art*
Je m'intéresse surtout à l'art abstrait.
I'm mainly interested in abstract art.

article m.   *article*
Je viens de lire un article au sujet de la situation politique de
    notre pays.
I just read an article about the political situation of our country.

ascenseur m.   *elevator*
Je ne prends jamais l'ascenseur, j'en ai peur!
I never take the elevator; I'm scared of it!

aspirateur m.   *vacuum*
Il passe l'aspirateur avant de faire la lessive.
He's vacuuming before doing the laundry.

asseoir, s'   *to sit down*
Vous pouvez vous asseoir.
You may sit down.

assez de   *enough (of)*
Je n'ai pas assez de farine pour cette recette.
I don't have enough flour for this recipe.

assister à   *to attend*
Normalement elles assistent à la messe du samedi soir parce
    qu'elle est moins longue que celle du dimanche matin.
*Normally they attend the Saturday night mass because it's shorter than
    the one on Sunday morning.*

assumer   *to assume, to take on*
Désormais il va assumer toutes les responsabilités.
From now on he's going to take on all responsibilities.

assurance f.   *insurance*
Elle n'a pas d'assurance maladie.
She doesn't have health insurance.

assurer   *to assure, to insure*
Je peux vous assurer que notre entreprise fera face à cette crise.
I can assure you that our company will handle this crisis.

astreindre   *to compel, to force*
Cette nouvelle nous astreint à repenser notre projet.
This piece of news compels us to rethink our project.

atout m.   *asset, advantage, trump card*
Ce diplôme sera un atout professionnel quand vous chercherez
   du travail.
This degree will be a professional asset when you look for work.

attentat m.   *attack, assassination attempt*
L'attentat a eu lieu hier. Heureusement personne n'a été blessé.
The attack was yesterday. Luckily no one was hurt.

attention f.   *attention*
Le prof attire l'attention de la classe sur les devoirs pour mercredi.
The professor draws the class's attention to the assignments due
   Wednesday.

attention f. (exclamation)   *attention, care*
Attention!
Watch out!

attirer   *to attract*
Je pense que ce nouveau café va attirer beaucoup d'attention.
I think that this new café will attract a lot of attention.

aubaine f.   *windfall, a argain, godsend*
Quelle aubaine! On a eu notre nouvelle voiture pour pas cher.
What a godsend! We got our new car at a bargain price.

aucun(e)   *none*
Aucun étudiant n'est prêt pour l'examen.
No student is ready for the test.

aujourd'hui   *today*
Elles partent aujourd'hui pour deux semaines en Tunisie.
They're leaving today for two weeks in Tunisia.

auparavant   *beforehand, previously*
Hier j'ai fait la connaissance de quelqu'un que je ne connaissais
   pas auparavant.
Yesterday I met someone that I didn't know previously.

aussi   *also, too*
On va visiter Rennes, Rouen et Quimper aussi, si on a le temps.
We're going to visit Rennes, Rouen, and Quimper, too, if we have the time.

autant de   *so much / so many*
Je n'ai jamais eu autant de cadeaux pour mon anniversaire!
I have never had so many gifts for my birthday!

autocar m.   *intercity bus, coach*
Au lieu de prendre le train, je préfère voyager en autocar.
Instead of taking the train, I prefer to take the intercity bus.

autorité f.   *authority*
Vous n'avez pas l'autorité de prendre cette décision.
You don't have the authority to make this decision.

autoroute f.   *highway*
Les camionneurs préfèrent rouler sur les autoroutes la nuit quand
   il y a peu de circulation.
*Truck drivers prefer to drive on highways at night when there is not
   much traffic.*

autour de   *around, about*
Le vendredi soir ma famille et moi faisons une promenade autour
   de la Place St. Marc.
*On Friday nights my family and I take a walk around St. Marc's
   Square.*

autre   *other, another*
Je peux voir une autre couleur, s'il vous plaît?
May I see another color, please?

autres, les   *the rest, the others*
Vous pouvez venir chez moi mais les autres doivent
   rester ici.
You can come to my place but the others must stay here.

autrui m.   *others, other people*
Vous avez un très bon jugement sur autrui.
You have very good judgment about other people.

avaler   *to swallow*
Il est difficile d'avaler ces gros comprimés!
It's hard to swallow these big pills!

avant de   *before*
Tu devrais lire le livre avant de le critiquer!
You should read the book before criticizing it!

avantage m. *advantage*
De nos jours parler plusieurs langues est vraiment un avantage
   pour ceux qui veulent travailler dans un contexte international.
*Nowadays, speaking several languages is a real advantage for people
   who wish to work in an international context.*

avec *with*
Est-ce qu'ils veulent travailler avec nous?
Do they want to work with us?

avenue f. *avenue*
L'avenue des Champs-Elysées est bien connue dans le monde entier.
The Avenue of the Champs-Elysées is well known the world over.

avertir *to warn, notify*
La banque va nous avertir quand notre hypothèque sera acceptée.
The bank will notify us when our mortgage is approved.

avertissement m. *warning, notification*
Il vient de nous donner l'avertissement que notre immeuble sera
   bientôt vendu.
He just gave us notification that our building soon will be sold.

aveugle *blind*
Il paraît que notre vieil oncle devient de plus en plus aveugle.
It appears that our elderly uncle is becoming more and more blind.

avion m. *airplane*
L'agent de voyage nous recommande de voyager par avion.
The travel agent recommends that we travel by airplane.

avoir *to have*
Ce soir je vais avoir quelques amies chez moi pour une petite fête.
Tonight I'm going to have a few friends over for a small party.

avouer *to admit*
Je dois avouer que mes enfants n'ont jamais mangé de chocolat!
I must admit that my kids have never eaten chocolate!

B

bac m. *baccalaureate degree that permits one to enter the university
   system in France.*
Elle a échoué au bac donc elle doit retenter l'examen l'année
   prochaine.
She failed the bac exam, so she has to retry the exam next year.

bâcler   *to botch*
L'artiste n'a pas fait attention et il a bâclé son ouvrage.
The artist didn't pay attention and botched his work.

badaud m.   *curious onlooker, rubbernecker*
Malheureusement, les accidents de voiture attirent les badauds.
Unfortunately, car accidents attract curious onlookers.

badiner   *to joke, to take something likely*
Comme il badine constamment on ne sait jamais s'il est sérieux.
Since he's always joking, we never know if he's serious.

bafouiller   *to fumble for one's words*
Au début il était si nerveux qu'il bafouillait mais ça va mieux
maintenant.
*In the beginning he was so nervous that he fumbled for his words, but
he's much better now.*

bagage m.   *bag, baggage*
On peut laisser nos bagages à la consigne, n'est-ce pas?
We can leave our bags at the baggage checkroom, right?

bagarre f.   *fight, scuffle*
Tu vas te faire exclure de cet établissement si tu n'arrêtes pas
toutes ces bagarres.
*You're going to be expelled from this school if you don't stop all of these
fights.*

bagarrer, se   *to fight*
Il est tellement agressif qu'il se bagarre avec tout le monde.
He's so aggressive that he fights with everyone.

bagatelle f.   *trifle, small matter*
Il parlait de son problème comme si ce n'était qu'une bagatelle.
He was talking about his problem as if it was only a small matter.

bague f.   *ring*
Tiens! Hier j'ai retrouvé la bague que j'avais perdue il y a un an!
Hey! Yesterday I found the ring that I had lost a year ago!

baiser, donner un m.   *to give a kiss*
Chaque matin ma mère me donne un baiser avant d'aller au travail.
Each morning my mom gives me a kiss before leaving for work.

baisser *to lower*
Baisse tes phares quand tu conduis ici, sinon tu vas aveugler les autres conducteurs.
Lower your headlights when you drive here; if you don't, you'll blind the other drivers.

bal m. *a ball, dance*
Tu as besoin de trouver un bon déguisement pour le bal masqué.
You need to find a good costume for the costume ball.

balader, se *to go for a stroll*
J'aime bien me balader quand je me sens stressé pour me détendre.
I like to go for a stroll when I am feeling stressed in order to relax.

balbutier *mumble, to stammer*
Le petit gamin apprend à parler donc il balbutie beaucoup.
The little child is learning to talk so he stammers a lot.

balle f. *bullet*
On a trouvé des balles dans le champ derrière la maison de nos grand-parents.
We found some bullets in the field behind our grandparents' house.

banal(e) *commonplace, ordinary, unoriginal, uninteresting*
Les commentaires de notre collègue étaient assez banals.
Our colleague's commentaries were pretty unoriginal.

banaliser *to make commonplace, to trivialize*
Le phénomène de mode banalise l'emploi de ce terme.
The use of this term is becoming commonplace now.

banane f. *banana*
Normalement mon fils prend une banane et des biscuits pour le goûter.
Normally as an afterschool snack my son has a banana and a few cookies.

bande dessinée f. *comic book, comic strip*
comic strip
Les bandes dessinées sont beaucoup plus populaires en France qu'aux États-Unis.
Comic books are much more popular in France than they are in the United States.

banlieue f. *suburb*
Le jeune couple rêve de quitter la banlieue.
The young couple dreams about getting out of the suburbs.

bannir   *to banish*
Le gouvernement bannit ces criminels de notre pays.
The government is banishing these criminals from our country.

banque f.   *bank*
Sandrine vient d'ouvrir un compte d'épargne à la banque dont
   on parlait hier.
*Sandrine just opened a savings account at the bank we were talking
   about yesterday.*

banqueroute f.   *bankruptcy (criminal)*
Le PDG essaie d'éviter de mentionner le mot "banqueroute"
   devant les investisseurs.
*The CEO is trying to avoid mentioning the word "bankruptcy" in front
   of the investors.*

baraque f.   *shack, dump*
Quelle baraque! J'ai horreur de cette maison.
What a dump! I hate this house.

baratin m.   *snow job, sweet talk, smooth talk, bunk*
Et me voilà encore une fois séduit par son baratin!
And here I am once again, taken in by his sweet talk!

barbe f.   *beard*
Je trouve cet homme à la barbe blanche dégoûtant.
I find this man with the white beard disgusting.

bas(se)   *low*
Le plafond dans ce salon est un peu trop bas à mon avis.
The ceiling in this living room is a bit too low, in my opinion.

bas (en)   *downstairs, below*
Attendez-nous en bas, s'il vous plaît.
Please wait for us downtairs.

basculer   *to tip over, to topple; to change dramatically*
Sa vie a basculé le jour où elle a découvert son cancer.
Her life changed dramatically the day she discovered her cancer.

bateau m.   *boat*
L'année dernière on a pris le bateau Sète-Maroc. Quel voyage
   inoubliable!
*Last year we took the boat from Sète to Morocco. What an unforgettable
   trip!*

bâtiment m.   *building*
Mon beau-frère est l'architecte de tous les bâtiments dans ce quartier.
My brother-in-law is the architect of all the buildings in this neighborhood.

bavarder   *to chatter, to gossip*
Les deux élèves n'arrêtaient pas de bavarder pendant le cours.
The two pupils didn't stop chattering during class.

baver   *to drool, to salivate, to leak*
Les bijoux de cette marque font baver toutes les jeunes actrices à Hollywood en ce moment.
This brand of jewelry is making all the young actresses in Hollywood drool at the moment.

beau(belle) (**bel** in front of a vowel and *h*)   *beautiful*
Quel beau chat!
What a beautiful cat!
Quelle belle idée!
What a beautiful idea!
Quel bel hôtel!
What a beautiful hotel!

beaucoup   *a lot*
Il faut avoir beaucoup de patience avec les enfants.
It's necessary to have a lot of patience with children.

bégayer   *to stammer, to stutter*
On sait tout de suite quand notre prof est nerveux parce qu'il commence à bégayer.
We know right away when our teacher is nervous because he starts to stammer.

béguin m.   *infatuation, crush*
Pratiquement tous les garçons de notre classe ont le béguin pour ma copine Estelle.
Practically all the boys in our class have a crush on my friend Estelle.

berner   *to fool, to deceive*
Le Chat botté décide de berner le roi et d'enrichir son maître.
Puss in Boots decides to fool the king and gain riches for his master.

besogne f.   *labor, drudgery*
Ce travail difficile représente une grande besogne pour nous.
This difficult job is truly a drudgery for us.

besoin m.   *need*
On a besoin de faire la lessive avant de faire nos valises.
We need to do the laundry before we pack our suitcases.

besoin de, avoir   *to need*
Ils ont besoin d'aller à la banque avant qu'elle ne ferme.
They need to go to the bank before it closes.

bestiole f.   *creepy-crawly*
Il a horreur des bestioles!
He's terrified of creepy-crawlies!

bête   *stupid, dumb*
Parfois je te trouve vraiment bête, tu sais.
You know, sometimes I think you're really stupid.

bête f.   *animal, beast*
As-tu vu La Belle et la Bête de Cocteau? C'est le film préféré de
    mon père.
Have you seen Cocteau's Beauty and the Beast? It's my dad's favorite film.

bêtise f.   *stupidity*
Si elle a la bêtise de penser que ses profs vont la croire, alors elle
    délire!
*If she has the stupidity to think that her teachers are going to believe
    her, then she's crazy!*

bêtise, faire une f.   *gaffe, to do something stupid*
Tu viens de faire une bêtise, excuse-toi!
You just did something stupid. Say you're sorry!

béton m.   *concrete*
Je trouve ce quartier déprimant! Tous les immeubles sont en
    béton.
*This neighborhood is depressing! All the apartment buildings are made
    of concrete.*

beurre m.   *butter*
Achetons du beurre à la crémerie.
Let's buy some butter at the dairy store.

bibliothèque f.   *library*
Si tu passais plus de temps à la bibliothèque, tu aurais plus de
    succès dans tes cours, tu sais.
*If you spent more time at the library, you would have more success in
    your courses, you know.*

bichonner *to dress up, to pamper*
Maxime bichonne son copain, il a tout ce qu'il veut!
Maxime pampers his boyfriend, he has everything he wants.

bidon m. *phony, hogwash*
C'est du bidon, oublie ce qu'il te dit.
It's hogwash, forget what he tells you.

bidule m. *thingamajig, thingie*
Où est le petit bidule que j'avais mis ici l'autre jour?
Where's that little thingie I put here the other day?

bien *well*
Elle écrit bien le grec mais elle a du mal à le parler.
She writes Greek well but has difficulty speaking it.

bien que *although*
Bien que je me sois amélioré, je n'ai pas progressé autant que je
l'aurais espéré.
Although I've improved, I haven't progressed as much as I would've liked.

bientôt *soon*
Ils auront bientôt suffisament d'argent pour acheter une
maisonnette à la campagne.
They'll soon have enough money to buy a small cottage in the country.

bienvenu(e) *welcome*
Madame Siméon, soyez la bienvenue!
Welcome, Madame Siméon!

bijou(x) m. (pl.) *jewel, gem*
Ce livre est un vrai bijou.
This book really is a gem.
Je viens de retrouver les bijoux de mon arrière-grand-mère, ils
sont incroyables!
I just found my great grandmother's jewels. They're incredible!

bilan m. *balance sheet, outcome, toll*
Le comptable prépare le bilan de notre service.
The accountant is preparing the balance sheet for our department.
Le bilan de ce séisme sera très lourd à supporter pour ce pays.
The toll of the earthquake will be quite difficult for this country to deal with.

billet m. *ticket*
S'il te faut un billet pas cher, je te conseille de chercher sur Internet.
If you need a cheap ticket, I advise you to look on the Internet.

biscornu(e) *quirky*
On l'aime bien mais parfois elle a l'esprit biscornu.
We like her, but sometimes she's really quirky.

bistrot, bistro m. *café, pub, small restaurant*
Je veux te présenter à mes amis qui travaillent dans le bistrot du coin.
I want to introduce you to my friends who work in the small restaurant on the corner.

bizutage m. *hazing*
Suite à plusieurs incidents de bizutage, ce groupe a été banni de notre campus.
After several hazing incidents, this group has been banned from campus.

blafard(e) *pale*
Tu es un peu blafard, Michel. Tu es malade?
You are a bit pale, Michael. Are you sick?

blague f. *joke*
Il leur raconte toujours des blagues ridicules.
He always tells them ridiculous jokes.

blairer, ne pas pouvoir *(colloquial) to not be able to stand or tolerate someone*
Je peux pas blairer ce type!
I can't stand this guy!

blanc(-he) *white*
La mariée portait une robe blanche.
The bride wore a white dress.

blanchir *to whiten, to bleach*
On va essayer de blanchir cette chemise jaunie.
We're going to try to whiten this yellowed blouse.

bled m. *(colloquial) home village, town*
C'est où ton bled?
Where is your hometown?

blesser *to hurt, to injure, to wound*
Le soldat a été blessé pendant la guerre.
The soldier was wounded during the war.

bleu(e) *blue*
Ne mets pas un cardigan bleu avec cette robe rouge, ça cloche!
Don't wear a blue cardigan with this red dress. It clashes!

bloc-notes m.   *notepad*
Donne-moi un autre bloc-notes pour que je puisse laisser un
   message à mon colloc.
Give me another notepad so I can leave a message for my
   roommate.

bof!   *Whatever! I don't care.*
Tu sais, Marie ne sort plus avec Léon....Bof!
You know, Marie isn't going out with Léon any more....I don't care!

boire   *to drink*
Le médecin m'a dit de boire moins de gin et plus d'eau.
The doctor told me to drink less gin and more water.

bois m.   *wood, the woods*
Ma mère vient de fabriquer une cabane à oiseaux tout en bois.
My mom just made a birdhouse entirely out of wood.
L'après-midi on aime bien se promener dans les bois derrière
   notre maison.
We like to take walks in the woods behind our house every
   afternoon.

boiser   *to plant trees*
Le club écolo de notre école collecte de l'argent pour pouvoir
   boiser dans ce pré l'été prochain.
Our school's ecology club is fundraising to be able to plant trees in this
   meadow next summer.

boisson f.   *drink, beverage*
Quel est ta boisson préférée?
What's your favorite drink?

boîte f.   *box, can*
Tu peux acheter une boîte de sardines à l'épicerie?
Can you buy a can of sardines at the corner store?

bon(-ne)   *good*
Elle a un très bon ordinateur.
She has a very good computer.
J'espère que tu passeras une bonne journée à la foire.
I hope you have a good day at the fair.

bon marché   *cheap, low-cost, inexpensive*
Il a eu ses chaussures à bon marché.
He got his shoes for an inexpensive price.

bondir   *to leap*
On a bondi de joie après avoir entendu le résultat du match.
We jumped for joy when we heard the result of the game.

bonnet m.   *a winter hat*
J'ai décidé de tricoter un bonnet pour mon amie Barbara.
I decided to knit a hat for my friend Barbara.

bordel m.   *(colloquial) literally, a bordello; figuratively, a dump*
Quel bordel!
What a dump!

bordélique   *(colloquial) messy, chaotic*
Mon appart est tellement bordélique que je veux pas retourner chez moi!
My apartment is so messy that I can't stand to go home!

bordure f.   *border, edge*
On a garé notre voiture en bordure de la fôret.
We parked our car at the edge of the forest.

borné(e)   *narrow-minded*
J'en ai marre des ces crétins bornés à la télé!
I'm so sick of these narrow-minded idiots on the TV!

borne f.   *terminal, mile marker*
La borne Internet est par là.
The Internet terminal is this way.

bosser   *to work hard*
Si tu veux réussir à l'examen, tu dois vraiment bosser.
If you want to pass the test, you have to really work hard.

bouche f.   *mouth*
Cette tarte me fait venir l'eau à la bouche!
This pie makes my mouth water!

bouchée f.   *mouthful*
J'ai pris une bouchée de ta tarte, elle est délicieuse!
I took a mouthful of your pie, it's delicious!

bouder   *to pout*
Quand on ne lui donne pas ce qu'il veut, il boude.
When he doesn't get what he want, he pouts.

bouffe f.   *(colloquial) food*
J'aime bien la bouffe ici.
I really like the food here.

bouffer   *(colloquial) to eat, to chow down*
Et si on bouffait avant de nous en aller?
How about if we eat before we leave?

bouleversement m.   *upheaval*
Peu de gens n'ont pas été touchés par le bouleversement
économique récent.
Few people haven't been affected by the recent economic upheaval.

bouquin m.   *book (familiar)*
On a acheté un vieux bouquin au marché aux puces.
We bought an old book at the flea market.

bourde f.   *blunder*
La nouvelle bourde de mon mari est très sérieuse.
My husband's newest blunder is quite serious.

bourré(e)   *filled, packed with, (colloquial) drunk, loaded*
Après trois heures au bar, ils sont complètement bourrés.
After three hours at the bar, they are completely loaded.

bourrique f.   *(colloquial) pig-headed person*
C'est une bourrique que tout le monde déteste.
He's a pig-headed person whom everyone hates.

bourse f.   *scholarship, grant*
Cet étudiant-là vient de recevoir une bourse d'études de notre
conseil d'administration.
*That student just got an educational scholarship from our board of
directors.*

bourse f.   *the stock exchange*
Ces actions ne sont pas cotées à la Bourse de New York.
These stocks aren't listed on the New York Stock Exchange.

bousculer   *to push, to jostle*
Il y a tellement de passants dans la rue que tout le monde est
bousculé par la foule.
*There are so many people on the street that everyone is jostled by the
crowd.*

bouteille f.   *bottle*
Ils ont acheté trois bouteilles de vin blanc pour la fête.
They bought three bottles of white wine for the party.

bracelet m. *bracelet*
Elle est triste parce qu'elle a perdu son nouveau bracelet.
She's sad because she lost her new bracelet.

branché(e) *(colloquial) in the know, cool*
Elle vient de s'installer dans un quartier vraiment branché.
She just moved into a really cool neighborhood.

bras m. *arm*
Depuis le match de rugby d'hier, Jean-Claude a vraiment mal
   au bras.
Jean-Claude's arm really hurts since yesterday's rugby match.

bredouiller *to speak unclearly*
Nous ne la comprenons pas parce qu'elle bredouille tout le temps.
We don't understand her because she speaks unclearly all the time.

bref *in short*
Bref, on a eu toutes sortes de problèmes.
In short, we had all sorts of problems.

brevet m. *patent; diploma*
Il est en train de préparer un brevet technique dans un établisse-
   ment près de chez lui.
He's in the midst of earning a technical degree at a school nearby.

bricoler *to putter around, to tinker*
Mon grand-père passe des heures à bricoler dans son jardin.
My grandfather spends hours puttering around in his garden.

bricolage m. *DIY, do-it-yourself hobbies*
Pour completer ce projet on a dû faire du bricolage.
To complete this project we had to do a bit of DIY.

brièvement *briefly, brief*
Explique-moi brièvement ton problème!
Give me a brief explanation of your problem.

brosse f. *brush*
Ça fait quatre jours que j'ai perdu ma nouvelle brosse, tu l'as vue
   quelque part?
I lost my new brush four days ago. Have you seen it anywhere?

brouillard m. *fog*
L'avion n'a pas pu atterrir à cause du brouillard.
The plane wasn't able to land because of the fog.

brouiller   *to blur, to confuse*
Toutes ces informations brouillaient mes idées.
All of this information confused me.

bruit m.   *noise*
On a soudainement eu peur parce qu'on a entendu un bruit fort à l'extérieur.
We suddenly became scared because we heard a loud noise outside.

brûler   *to burn*
Sandra va dîner au restaurant parce que Mathias a brûlé leur repas.
Sandra is going to have dinner at the restaurant because Mathias burnt their meal.

brûlure f.   *burn*
J'ai une brûlure sur le cou et ça fait mal!
I have a burn on my neck and it hurts!

brume f.   *mist*
Cette brume nous empêche de voir devant nous.
This mist is preventing us from seeing in front of us.

brun(e)   *brown*
Mon père est brun et sa mère était brune aussi.
My dad has brown hair, and his mother was a brunette as well.

brushing m.   *blow-out*
Je vais chez mon coiffeur une fois par semaine pour un brushing.
I go to my hairdresser once a week for a blow-out.

brusque   *abrupt, sudden*
Je n'apprécie pas votre ton brusque, Mademoiselle.
I don't appreciate your abrupt tone, Miss.

brusquement   *abruptly, suddenly*
Tout le monde riait quand brusquement Jean a commencé à pleurer.
Everyone was laughing, when suddenly Jean started crying.

brutalité f.   *brutality*
Les citoyens de ce pays craignent la brutalité de leur roi.
The citizens of this country fear the brutality of their king.

bruyant(e)   *noisy, loud*
Il est très bruyant comme bébé, il ne se tait jamais.
He's a very noisy baby—he's never quiet.

bruyère f.   *heather*
Les collines derrière notre petite maison sont couvertes de
     bruyère, c'est très joli.
*The hills behind our little house are covered with heather. It's quite
     beautiful.*

bûche f.   *log*
Maman va bientôt servir notre bûche de Noël annuelle, miam
     miam!
Mom soon is going to serve our annual Yule log cake. Yum yum!

budget m.   *budget*
J'utilise un nouveau logiciel qui m'aide à contrôler notre budget
     familial.
I'm using a new software that's helping me control our family budget.

bureau m.   *office*
Elle travaille tard et ne quitte jamais le bureau avant onze heures
     du soir.
She works late and never leaves the office before eleven o'clock at night.

buriner   *to engrave*
On a trouvé une boîte burinée à la brocante qui est vraiment
     jolie.
*We found an engraved box at the flea market that is really
     pretty.*

bus m.   *local bus*
Pour aller chez Ahmed il faut prendre au moins deux bus
     différents.
To go to Ahmed's place, you have to take at least two different buses.

but m.   *goal, purpose*
Je ne vois pas très bien le but de cette question, que veux-tu
     savoir exactement?
*I don't really understand the point of this question—what do you want
     to know exactly?*

buter   *to bump into, to trip over something; (colloquial) to bump
     someone off*
Elle a buté contre toutes tes affaires par terre.
She tripped over your things all over the floor.
L'agent de police prétend que cet homme a buté la victime.
The police inspector alleges that this man bumped off the victim.

C

ça   *that*
Ça, c'est mon livre préféré.
That's my favorite book.

cacahuète f.   *peanut*
Notre fils est allergique aux cacahuètes.
Our son is allergic to peanuts.

cache-cache m.   *hide-and-seek*
Jouons à cache-cache!
Let's play hide-and-seek.

cacher   *to conceal*
Elle a du mal à cacher ses sentiments.
She has a hard time hiding her feelings.

cacher, se   *to hide oneself, to go into hiding*
Comme je ne vais pas en classe ce matin, je me cache pour que
    mon prof ne me voie pas.
*Since I'm not going to class this morning, I'm hiding so that my
    professor doesn't see me.*

cadeau m.   *present*
Ils vont offrir un cadeau d'anniversaire à leur collègue qui fête
    ses 70 ans.
*They're going to give a birthday present to their colleague, who is
    celebrating her seventieth birthday.*

cadet(-ette)   *younger, youngest*
Mon frère cadet vient de fêter ses 21 ans.
My younger brother just celebrated his twenty-first birthday.

cadre m.   *frame, setting, framework; executive*
Mettons cette photo dans un cadre.
Let's put this picture in a frame.
Les cadres de cette entreprise sont bien payés.
The executives of this firm are well paid.

caduc(-uque)   *obsolete, nullified*
Cette pratique est caduque, ça ne se fait plus.
This practice is obsolete; it is no longer done.

cafard m.   *cockroach*
Leur appartement est infect, il y a des cafards partout.
Their apartment is disgusting; there are cockroaches everywhere.

cafard, avoir le   *to be depressed, down in the dumps*
J'ai le cafard aujourd'hui et je ne sais pas pourquoi.
I'm depressed today and I don't know why.

café m.   *coffee*
Si on prenait un café?
How about getting some coffee?

café m.   *café*
Il y a café charmant que tous les étudiants fréquentent. Tu veux y aller?
There's a chraming café that all the students go to. Do you want to go there?

cafétéria f.   *cafeteria*
On a fini par déjeuner à la cafeteria parce qu'on n'avait pas le temps d'aller au restaurant.
We ended up eating at the cafeteria because we didn't have the time to go to a restaurant.

cafouillage m.   *bungling, chaos, mess*
Suite aux tempêtes de neige, c'est le cafouillage total dans les aéroports de New York.
Because of the snowstorms, the New York–area airports are a total mess.

cahier m.   *workbook, notebook*
La classe doit faire trois exercices de grammaire dans le cahier pour demain.
The class has to do three grammar exercises in the workbook for tomorrow.

caisse f.   *cash register, checkout*
Avant de quitter le magasin, je dois régler à la caisse.
Before leaving the store, I have to pay at the cash register.

caissier(-ière) m. (f.)   *cashier, checkout employee*
Le weekend elle travaille comme caissière.
She works weekends as a cashier.

calculatrice f.   *calculator*
Je suis nulle en maths donc je me sers toujours d'une calculatrice.
I'm terrible at math so I always use a calculator.

caler   *to wedge, to prop up; to fill up, to give in*
Mettons cette boîte ici pour caler l'étagère.
Let's put this box here to prop up the bookcase.

calfeutrer, se   *to hide away*
Le weekend on se calfeutre dans notre maison.
On weekends we hide away in our house.

calme   *calm*
C'est bizarre que la mer soit si calme après tant d'orages.
It's odd that the sea is co calm after so many storms.

calmer, se   *to calm oneself, to calm down*
Calmez-vous Madame, vous n'avez pas à vous inquiéter!
Calm down, ma'am, you don't need to get so worried!

caméra f.   *video or movie camera*
Le couple a acheté une caméra pour filmer sa lune de miel.
The couple bought a video camera to film their honeymoon.

camion m.   *truck*
Quand ma sœur était petite, elle jouait sans cesse avec un petit camion vert.
When my sister was little, she played non-stop with a little green truck.

campagne f.   *the countryside*
Moi je préfère la montagne à la campagne.
Personally, I prefer the mountains to the countryside.

canapé m.   *couch, sofa*
On a acheté ce canapé-là à un très bon prix.
We bought this couch for a really good price.

cancre m.   *dunce*
Cet étudiant-là est vraiment le cancre de la classe.
That student is really the dunce of the class.

canicule f.   *heat wave*
On souffre de la canicule depuis deux semaines.
We have been suffering from a heat wave for two weeks.

canon   *(colloquial) great, gorgeous*
Sa nouvelle voiture est vraiment canon!
His new car is really great!

capital m.   *capital*
Malheureusement elle n'a pas suffisament de capital pour monter son affaire.
Unfortunately she doesn't have enough capital to start her business.

capitale f.   *capital city*
Quelle est la capitale de la France?
What is the capital of France?

capiteux(-euse)   *heady, intoxicating*
Je trouve ce parfum vraiment capiteux.
I find this perfume truly intoxicating.

capituler   *to capitulate*
Après de longues discussions, le conseil a capitulé devant les
    demandes des employés.
*After long discussions, the board capitulated to the workers'
    demands.*

caprice m.   *whim; tantrum*
C'est un homme qui est complètement guidé par ses caprices.
He's a man who is completely guided by his whims.
Cet enfant fait un caprice chaque fois que l'on lui dit "non".
This child has a tantrum every time we tell him "No."

capricieux(-ieuse)   *capricious, temperamental*
Notre machine à laver est capricieuse; elle ne marche quasiment
    jamais!
Our washing machine is temperamental; it basically never works!

capter   *to pick up, to catch*
Mon portable ne capte jamais de signal.
My cellphone never picks up a signal.

captivant(e)   *enthralling, captivating*
Elle a joué une pièce de musique dont j'oublie le titre, mais c'était
    captivant.
*She played a piece of music whose title I forget, but it was
    enthralling.*

car m.   *intercity bus*
Au lieu de prendre le train, je préfère voyager en car.
Instead of taking the train, I prefer to travel by bus.

car   *because, as, for*
Je dois passer par le guichet car je suis à sec!
I need to stop by the cash machine because I'm broke!

carburer   *(colloquial) to run on, to function on*
Moi je carbure au café!
I run on coffee!

carnet m.   *book of tickets, notebook*
Comme vous êtes à Paris pour seulement une journée, vous
    devriez acheter un carnet de dix tickets.
*Since you're only in Paris for one day, you should buy a book of ten
    tickets.*

carrefour m.   *crossroads, intersection, forum*
La France est le carrefour de l'Europe.
France is the crossroads of Europe.
On organise un carrefour d'idées lors de notre congrès.
We are organizing a forum to be held at the time of our convention.

carrière f.   *career*
Mon neveu ne sait pas du tout ce qu'il veut faire comme
    carrière.
My nephew doesn't know at all what he wants to do for a career.

cartable m.   *school bag, satchel*
Mets tes fournitures dans ton nouveau cartable!
Put your school supplies in your school bag!

carte f.   *card, map, menu*
J'ai envoyé une carte de vœux à mon ancien prof.
I sent a greeting card to my former teacher.
Donne-moi la carte pour que je te montre notre ville.
Give me the map so I can point out our town.
Il n'y a rien sur la carte qui m'intéresse.
There is nothing on the menu that interests me.

cartonner   *to score, to nail it; to blow it*
Elle a eu une bonne note à l'examen? Oui, elle a cartonné!
She got a good grade on the test? Yes, she nailed it!
Oh bravo, t'as vraiment cartonné!
Congrats, you really blew it!

cartouche f.   *cartridge, carton*
Achète-moi des cartouches d'encre à la papeterie.
Buy me some ink cartridges at the stationery store.
Achetons une cartouche de cigarettes—c'est moins cher.
Let's buy a carton of cigarettes—it's less expensive.

cas m.   *case*
L'inspecteur va continuer son enquête même si l'affaire est close.
*The inspector is going to continue his inquiry even if the case is
    closed.*

caser   *to stick something somewhere, to find a place or spot for*
Heureusement le directeur a pu caser tous les stagiaires.
Luckily the director was able to find a spot for all the trainees.

casque m.   *helmet*
Elle ne permet pas à ses enfants de faire du vélo sans casque.
She doesn't let her kids ride their bikes without a helmet.

cassé(e)   *broke, broken*
Elle s'est cassé le bras en faisant du ski alpin.
She broke her arm while downhill skiing.

casse-croûte m.   *snack*
Veux-tu du jus d'orange avec ton casse-croûte?
Do you want some orange juice with your snack?

casser   *to break*
Il s'est cassé le bras en skiant.
He broke his arm while skiing.

cathédrale f.   *cathedral*
La cathédrale de Reims est un vrai joyau de l'art gothique.
The Reims cathedral is a real jewel of gothic architecture.

catholique   *Catholic*
L'Italie est un pays très catholique.
Italy is a very Catholic country.

cauchemar m.   *nightmare*
Hier soir mon mari a été réveillé brusquement par un cauchemar.
Last night my husband was abruptly awakened by a nightmare.

cauchemardesque   *nightmarish*
Notre viste chez ma belle-mère a été absolumment
     cauchemardesque.
Our visit to my mother-in-law's was absolutely nightmarish.

causer   *to cause*
Qu'est-ce qui a causé tous ces problèmes?
What has caused all these problems?

causer   *to chat*
Causons de nos inquiétudes pour que l'on se sente mieux.
Let's talk about our troubles so we feel better.

cautionner   *to give strong support to, to post bail*
Le president veut-il cautionner cette loi injuste?
Does the president wish to give his strong support to this unjust law?

ce, cette, ces (cet *in front of a vowel*)   *this, these*
Ce chat / cette maison/ cet homme / est adorable comme tout.
This cat/house/man is adorable as anything.
Ces tasses à café doivent être rangées dans le placard.
These coffee cups need to be put away in the cupboard.

ceinture f.   *belt*
Mets ta a ceinture de sécurité sinon tu risques d'avoir une
     amende.
Put on your seat belt or you might get a fine.

célèbre   *famous, well-known*
Phèdre est la pièce la plus célèbre de Racine.
Phèdre is Racine's most famous play.

célibataire   *single*
Je ne suis pas marié; je préfère rester célibataire.
I'm not married; I prefer to stay single.

celle(s)   *the one, those*
Celle qui arrivera en premier gagnera une récompense.
The one who arrives (there) first will win a prize.

celui(ceux)   *the one, those*
Tu préfères celui en vert ou celui en orange?
Do you prefer the green one or the orange one?
Ceux qui n'auront pas fini leurs devoirs n'auront pas le droit de
     sortir ce soir.
*Those who haven't finished their assignments won't have the right to go
     out tonight.*

censé(e)   *supposed to, presumed to*
Ils sont censés parler au carrefour demain, mais je ne crois pas
     qu'ils viennent.
*They are supposed to speak at the forum tomorrow, but I don't think
     they'll come.*

centre-ville m.   *downtown*
Et si on faisait du lèche-vitrine au centre-ville?
How about some window-shopping downtown?

céréales f. pl.   *grains, cereal*
Le matin, elle mange des céréales et un yaourt.
In the morning, she has cereal and a yogurt.

certain(e)   *certain, sure, definite*
Cet homme-là est méchant, c'est certain, mais parfois il est aussi
    très généreux.
That man is mean, that's for sure, but sometimes he's also quite
    generous.

certainement   *certainly, for certain*
On arrivera certainement avant toi.
We'll certainly arrive before you.

cesser   *to stop*
Elle est tellement bavarde, elle ne cesse de parler.
She's so talkative, she never stops speaking.

chacun(e)   *each one*
Il faut donner le même examen à chacun.
You have to give the same exam to each one.

chaise f.   *chair*
Je trouve que cette chaise rouge na va pas du tout dans ce salon
    bleu.
I think that this red chair doesn't go at all with this blue living room.

chaleur f.   *heat*
Quelle chaleur! Allons à la piscine.
What heat! Let's go to the pool.

chaleureux(-euse)   *warm, friendly*
On nous a fait un accueil très chaleureux à la réception de notre
    hôtel.
We were given a very friendly welcome at our hotel reception.

chambard m.   *din*
Le chambard ici m'empêche de lire mon bouquin.
The din here is preventing me from reading my book.

chambouler   *to flummox, mess up*
L'accident m'a complètement chamboulé!
The accident has completely messed me up!

chambre f.   *bedroom*
Quand Sandra était petite, elle partageait sa chambre avec ses
    deux petites sœurs.
When Sandra was little, she shared her room with her two younger
    sisters.

chambrer   *to bring to room temperature*
Il faut chambrer ce vin avant de le servir.
It's necessary to bring this wine to room temperature before serving it.

champ m.   *field*
L'agriculteur est dans son champ en train de planifier les prochaines récoltes.
The farmer is in his field planning his next crops.

chance f.   *luck*
Décidemment tu n'as pas de chance!
Clearly you have bad luck!

changement m.   *change, alteration*
Après plusieurs changements, l'éditeur a décidé de publier mon roman.
After several changes, the editor decided to publish my novel.

changer   *to changer*
Est-il jamais possible de vraiment changer quelqu'un?
Is it ever really possible to change someone?

chanson f.   *song*
Les chansons de Serge Gainsbourg sont un peu coquines, non?
Serge Gainsbourg's songs are a little naughty, aren't they?

chanter   *to sing*
Je ne chante que sous la douche.
I only sing in the shower.

chapeau(x) m. (pl.)   *hat*
J'ai envie de porter ce chapeau en feutre aujourd'hui.
I feel like wearing this felt hat today.

charabia m.   *mumbo jumbo, jibberish*
Tu comprends ce qu'il veut dire? Non, c'est du charabia.
Do you understand what he means? No, it's jibberish.

charger   *to load, to give someone the responsibility of doing something*
Il est chargé de résoudre ces problèmes administratifs.
He's been put in charge of resolving these administrative problems.

château(x) m. (pl.)   *castle*
Si tu aimes bien l'architecture de la Renaissance, le château de
Chenonceaux est à ne pas manquer.
*If you're interested in Renaissance architecture, don't miss the Chenon-
ceaux castle.*

châtier   *to chastise, to punish*
Le maître a châtié ses élèves pour leur mauvais comportement.
The teacher punished his pupils for their bad behavior.

chatouiller   *to tickle*
Ne me chatouille pas—je déteste ça!
Don't tickle me—I hate it!

chaud(e)   *hot*
Attention! La poêle est encore chaude!
Careful, the skillet is still hot!

chauffer   *to warm, to heat up*
Si tu as faim, on peut chauffer de la soupe.
If you're hungry, we can heat up some soup.

chauffeur m.   *driver*
Mon petit cousin rêve de devenir chauffeur de camion.
My little cousin dreams about becoming a truck driver.

chaussettes f. pl.   *socks*
Elle porte rarement des chaussettes en été.
She rarely wears socks in the summer.

chauve   *bald*
Tu ne reconnaîtrais pas Paul parce qu'il est tout chauve en ce
moment, il s'est rasé la tête.
*You wouldn't recognize Paul because he's completely bald at the
moment; he shaved his head.*

chemin m.   *way, path, lane*
Le bon chemin est par là, n'est-ce pas?
This is the correct path, right?

chemin (de fer) m.   *railroad, railway*
Mon oncle ne voyage que par chemin de fer.
My uncle only travels by rail.

chemise f. *shirt*
Ne me dis pas que tu vas mettre cette chemise verte-ci avec ce
   pantalon rayé-là!
*Don't tell me you're going to wear this green shirt with those striped
   pants!*

chemisier m. *blouse*
Elle a l'air très professionnel habillée en tailleur noir et chemisier
   gris.
She looks very professional dressed in a black suit and a gray blouse.

chèque m.
Je peux régler par chèque?
Can I pay by check?

cher(chère) *dear, expensive*
Je vous présente mon très cher ami Philippe.
Allow me to introduce my very dear friend Phillip.
Ces bottes sont un peu chères, non?
These boots are rather expensive, aren't they?

chercher *to look for*
Je suis en train de chercher un nouvel appartement parce que je
   déteste mon coloc.
*I'm in the process of looking for a new apartment because I can't stand
   my roommate.*

cheveu(x) m. (pl.) *hair*
Il se brosse rarement les cheveux.
He rarely brushes his hair.

chevronné(e) *experienced, seasoned*
En tant que prof chevronné, j'ai l'impression d'avoir tout vu.
As a seasoned professor, I feel like I've seen it all.

chez *at the house or place of*
Vous dînez chez Isabelle, n'est-ce pas?
You're having dinner at Isabelle's, right?

chiffre m. *figure, number*
Le PDG n'est pas du tout satisfait du chiffre d'affaires qu'il vient
   d'annoncer.
*The CEO isn't at all satisfied with the sales figures that he just
   announced.*

choisir   *to choose*
On doit choisir une destination pour notre lune de miel.
We need to choose a destination for our honeymoon.

choix m.   *choice*
Le directeur de l'établissement n'a pas eu le choix: il a exclu cet
    étudiant du collège.
*The director of the school really didn't have a choice: he expelled the
    student from middle school.*

chômage, au m.   *unemployed*
Il est au chômage depuis trois ans.
He's been unemployed for three years.

choper   *(colloquial) to nab, to catch, to pick up*
Il a chopé une sacré toux pendant qu'il était en vacances.
He picked up a nasty cough while on vacation.

choquer   *to shock*
Les images violentes de l'attentat diffusées à la télé nous ont tous
    choqués.
The violent images of the attack, broadcast on TV, shocked us all.

chose f.   *thing*
Quelle est la chose dont tu as le plus peur?
What is the thing you're most afraid of?

chouette   *great, terrific*
On a retrouvé notre chat! Chouette!
We found our cat! Terrific!

chouïa m.   *a bit (colloquial)*
Donne-moi juste un chouïa de chocolat, s'il te plaît.
Give me just a bit of chocolate, please.

chuchoter   *to whisper*
Comme on parle un peu trop fort, la dame nous prie de chuchoter.
Since we're talking a bit too loudly, the woman is asking us to whisper.

ciel m.   *the sky, heaven*
Le ciel devient de plus en plus noir, il va certainement faire un orage.
The sky is becoming increasingly darker, it's certainly going to storm.

cinéma m.   *cinema, movie theater, film*
Je fais une étude historique du cinéma soviétique.
I'm doing a historical study of Soviet cinema.

cinoche m.   *(colloquial) the movies*
Et si on allait au cinoche?
How about going to the movies?

ciseaux m. pl.   *scissors*
Il ne faut pas laisser les enfants courir avec des ciseaux.
You shouldn't let children run with scissors.

clair(e)   *light, bright, clear*
L'eau dans ce lac est si claire que l'on peut voir le fond.
The water in this lake is so clear that you can see the bottom.

clamser   *(colloquial) to die*
Hier soir j'ai rêvé que tous mes amis avaient clamsé. C'était affreux!
Last night I dreamed that all my friends died. It was awful!

clandestin(e)   *underground, illegal*
La police est à la recherche de travailleurs clandestins.
The police are looking for illegal workers.

classe f.   *class*
Je dois aller en classe maintentant.
I have to go to class now.

clé/clef f.   *key*
Elle nous a laissé la clé sous le paillasson.
She left the key for us under the doormat.

client(e) m. (f.)   *client, customer*
Les clients de cette enterprise louche sont peu satisfaits.
The clients of this shady business are not very satisfied.

climat m.   *climate*
J'ai du mal à m'habituer au climat de ce pays.
I'm having trouble getting used to the climate of this country.

cloche f.   *bell*
On peut entendre la cloche de l'église d'ici.
We can hear the church bell from here.

cœur m.   *heart*
Je t'aime de tout mon cœur.
I love you with all my heart.

coiffer   *to do someone's hair*
Je lui demande de me coiffer.
I'm asking him to do my hair.

coiffer, se   *to do one's hair*
Elle ne se coiffe jamais avant de quitter la maison.
She never does her hair before leaving the house.

coin m.   *corner*
Notre maison est située au coin de la rue de la Fourchette et de
l'avenue de l'Opéra.
Our house is at the corner of Fourchette Street and Opéra Avenue.

coincé(e)   *stuck, backed into a corner*
Il a voulu me coincer pendant notre dispute mais il n'a pas pu.
He wanted to back me into a corner during our argument but couldn't.

colère, en f.   *angry*
Franck est un homme désagréable qui est tout le temps en colère.
Frank is a disagreeable man who is always angry.

colis m.   *parcel, package*
Un colis vient d'arriver pour toi.
A parcel just arrived for you.

collège m.   *middle school, junior high school*
Normalement les enfants de son âge vont au college, mais
comme Hamid est une tête il va au lycée.
*Normally kids his age go to middle school, but since Hamid is a star
student he's going to high school.*

coller   *to stick, to glue*
Les enfants sont en train de coller des étiquettes sur le mur, leur
mère va se fâcher!
*The children are putting stickers on the wall; their mom is going to get
angry about that!*

collier m.   *necklace*
Louis vient d'offrir un collier en or à sa mère pour son
anniversaire.
Louis just gave his mother a gold necklace for her birthday.

collision (entrer en)   *to collide*
Les deux voitures sont entrées en collision mais personne ne s'est
blessé.
The two cars collided, but no one was hurt.

combien   *How much?*
Ce bouquin coûte combien?
How much does this book cost?

comme   *as, since*
Comme tu es très impoli, je ne vais pas répondre à ta question.
As you're very impolite, I'm not going to answer your question.

commencer   *to start, to begin*
Dépêche-toi! Le film commence dans dix minutes!
Hurry up! The movie starts in ten minutes!

commode   *handy, useful, convenient*
Cet outil est très commode.
This tool is very handy.

compatissant(e)   *compassionate*
Je déteste mon médecin, il est peu compatissant.
I hate my doctor; he's not in the least bit compassionate.

complet(e)   *complete, full*
Comme l'hôtel est complet on doit chercher une chambre
    ailleurs.
Because this hotel is full, we have to look for a room elsewhere.

comprendre   *to understand*
J'ai du mal à comprendre son raisonnement.
I'm having a hard time understanding his reasoning.

compte m.   *account*
Avant de déménager je vais fermer mon compte en banque.
Before I move I'm going to close my bank account.

compter   *to count*
Je peux toujours compter sur Zac, c'est un mec très fiable.
I can always count on Zac; he's a really dependable guy.

conduire   *to drive*
Normalement les ados de New York ne savent pas conduire
    parce qu'ils n'en ont pas besoin.
*Normally, teenagers in New York City don't know how to drive, because
    they don't need to.*

conférence f.   *lecture, conference*
Les journalistes se rassemblent pour une conférence de presse
    avec le candidat.
The journalists are gathering for a press conference with the candidate.

confiture f.   *jam*
Cette confiture à la framboise est délicieuse.
This raspberry jam is delicious.

confondre *to confuse, to confound*
Ce problème confond les scientifiques depuis longtemps.
This problem has confounded scientists for a long time.

confortable *comfortable*
Notre lit n'est pas du tout confortable.
Our bed isn't comfortable at all.

confus(e) *confused, ashamed*
Je suis trop confus par son histoire pour pouvoir la raconter.
I'm too ashamed by his story to be able to tell it.

confusion f. *confusion*
Selon les reportages, la confusion règne dans la capitale après
l'attentat.
According to reports, confusion reigns in the capital after the attack.

congé m. *leave, time off*
Il part en congé pour cinq jours.
He's taking time off for five days.

conjoint(e) m. (f.) *spouse, partner*
Mon conjoint souffre de migraines.
My spouse suffers from migraines.

connaître *to know, to be familiar with*
Je connais beaucoup de gens qui ont ce même problème.
I know many people who have this same problem.

conseiller *to advise, to counsel*
Notre prof vient de nous conseiller de nous inscrire à son cours
de philo.
Our professor just advised us to enroll in his philosophy course.

constater *to notice, to note, to ascertain*
Depuis quelques semaines on constate une augmentation du
nombre de touristes.
For the past couple of weeks we have noticed a rise in the amount of tourists.

consulat m. *consulate*
Je dois récuper mon passeport au consulat avant qu'il ne ferme.
I need to pick up my passport at the consulate before it closes.

content(e) *happy*
Je suis content de faire votre connaissance.
I am happy to meet you.

continuer   *to continue*
Elle espère pouvoir continuer à écrire son blog lorsqu'elle sera à l'étranger.
She hopes to be able to continue writing her blog while she's abroad.

contraire   *opposite, contrary*
Tu fais toujours tout le contraire de ce que je te dis de faire.
You always do the exact opposite of what I tell you to do.

contre   *against*
Le sénateur se dit contre la nouvelle loi d'amnistie.
The senator says that he's against the new amnesty law.

copain (copine) m. (f.)   *friend, pal, boyfriend or girlfriend*
Ce soir il sort avec son copain Antoine.
Tonight he's going out with his friend Anthony.

copieux(-ieuse)   *hearty, copious*
Après notre repas copieux à l'auberge, on veut faire la sieste.
After our hearty meal at the inn, we want to take a nap.

corbeille f.   *basket*
Tu peux remplir la corbeille à pain avant le dîner?
Can you fill the bread basket before dinner?

corps m.   *body*
Les gens ne prennent pas assez soin de leurs corps.
People don't take good enough care of their bodies.

correct(e)   *correct, right, accurate*
Il parle un anglais correct.
He speaks correct English.

corriger   *to correct*
La maîtresse a besoin de corriger les interros de sa classe avant la fin de l'année scolaire.
The elementary school teacher needs to correct her classs' quizzes before the end of the school year.

cossu(e)   *plush, fancy*
Ils habitent dans un appartement cossu dans le quartier le plus cher de Paris.
They live in a plush apartment in the most expensive neighborhood of Paris.

costaud(e)   *(colloquial) beefy, sturdy, husky*
Cet homme costaud pourrait te casser la figure, donc fais gaffe!
This beefy guy could break your neck, so watch out!

côte f.   *coast*
On trouvé un gîte tout près de la côte.
We found a vacation rental quite close to the coast.

côté m.   *side*
Le café dont on a parlé est du côté de la librairie.
The café we were talking about is on the side of the bookstore.

côté, à...de   *next to*
Elle habite à côté de la pharmacie et en face de la boulangerie.
She lives next to the pharmacy and across from the bakery.

coton m.   *cotton*
Mets ta robe en coton pour la fête de ce soir.
Put on your cotton dress for the party tonight.

cou m.   *neck*
Je vais te tordre le cou!
I'm going to wring your neck!

coucher, se   *to go to bed*
Ils vont se coucher avant minuit parce qu'ils doivent se réveiller tôt.
They're going to bed before midnight because they have to get up early.

coudre   *to sew*
Il veut apprendre à coudre.
He wants to learn how to sew.

couler   *to flow, to sink*
J'aime bien son style; les idées coulent de manière très claire.
I like her writing; the ideas flow very clearly.
Tout le monde s'est noyé quand le bateau a coulé.
Everyone drowned when the boat sank.

couleur f.   *color*
De quelle couleur est leur nouvelle voiture?
What color is their new car?

coulisse, en f.   *backstage, behind the scenes*
Il préfère agir en coulisse plûtot qu'au grand jour.
He prefers to work behind the scenes rather than in broad daylight.

coup m.   *blow, hit*
Ces décisions prises à la hâte porteront un mauvais coup à sa fortune.
These hasty decisions will deal a blow to his fortune.

couper   *to cut*
Notre président a décidé de couper toute relation avec ce leader despotique.
Our president has decided to cut all official relations with this despotic leader.

courir   *to run*
Elle passe ses jours à courir après ses trois enfants.
She spends her days running after her three children.

courriel m.   *email*
Je viens de recevoir un courriel de mon grand-père, son premier!
I just got an email from my grandfather—his first ever!

courrier m.   *mail*
On attend toujours l'arrivée de notre courrier du jour.
We're still waiting for our daily mail delivery.

cours m.   *course, class*
Ce semestre je suis un cours de physique qui est vraiment ennuyeux.
This semester I'm taking a physics course that is truly boring.

court(e)   *short*
J'espère que mes cheveux pousseront parce que j'en ai marre d'avoir les cheveux courts.
I hope my hair grows because I'm fed up with having short hair.

couteau m.   *knife*
J'ai besoin d'un couteau pour notre partie de camping ce weekend.
I need a knife for our camping expedition this weekend.

coûter   *to cost*
Ces billets coûtent vraiment trop cher.
These tickets really cost too much.

coutume f.   *custom*
Je m'intéresse beaucoup aux coutumes de mariage de ce pays.
I'm very interested in the marriage customs of this country.

couvert(e)   *covered*
Le petit gamin est rentré de l'aire de jeux couvert de boue.
The little child came back from the playground covered in mud.

couverture f.   *cover, covering, blanket*
Regarde cette jolie couverture en patchwork que ma copine a
   faite pour moi.
Look at this pretty patchwork blanket my friend made for me.

couvrir   *to cover*
Il a suffisament d'argent pour couvrir toutes ses dettes.
He has enough money to cover all his debts.

crapaud m.   *toad; (colloquial) brat*
Il y a plein de crapauds dans notre petit jardin.
There are lots of toads in our little garden.
Je ne peux supporter leur fils, quel crapaud!
I can't stand their son—what a brat!

cravate f.   *necktie*
Tu dois absolumment mettre une cravate avec ce costume-là.
You definitely need to wear a tie with that suit.

crayon m.   *pencil*
Tu peux me prêter un crayon?
Can you lend me a pencil?

créer   *to create*
Il a décidé de créer son propre destin.
He decided to create his own destiny.

crevé(e)   *flat (tire); dead tired*
On a un pneu crevé, on doit le faire réparer.
We have a flat tire; we need to get it fixed.
Après notre journée à la plage, on était tous crevés.
After our day at the beach, we were all dead tired.

cri m.   *cry*
Le nouveau-né a poussé son premier petit cri du berceau.
The newborn gave its first little cry from the cradle.

crible, passer au   *to do a close examination, to go over with a*
   fine-tooth comb
Vous devriez passer cettre lettre au crible avant de l'envoyer.
You should go through this letter with a fine-tooth comb before
   sending it.

crime m.   *crime*
Cet homme a été condamné pour son crime.
This man was condemned for his crime.

crisper   *to become tense; to get on someone's nerves*
Ne te crispe pas, c'est pas grave!
Don't get tense, it's not a big deal!
Qu'est-ce qu'elle me crispe!
Oh, how she gets on my nerves!

croire   *to believe*
Elle ne veut pas nous croire.
She doesn't want to believe us.

croix f.   *cross*
En France les élèves n'ont pas le droit de porter des croix ou
   d'autres symboles religieux à l'école.
*In France, students aren't allowed to wear crosses or other religious
   symbols to school.*

cru(e)   *raw, uncooked*
Il vaut mieux manger des légumes crus autant que possible.
It's best to eat raw vegetables as much as possible

cuillère f.   *spoon*
Donne-moi une cuillère à soupe pour que je puisse manger.
Give me a soup spoon so I can eat.

cuir m.   *leather*
Malheureusement elle a décidé de porter un pantalon en cuir—
   quelle horreur!
Unfortunately she decided to wear leather pants—how awful!

cuisine f.   *cuisine, type of food*
Mon père est très friand de cuisine japonaise.
My dad is quite fond of Japanese food.

cuisine, faire la   *to cook*
Aujourd'hui les jeunes n'apprennent plus à faire la cuisine.
These days young peple are no longer learning to cook.

cuisinier(-ière) m. (f.)   *cook*
Ce café a besoin de trouver un autre cuisinier porce que celui-ci
   vient de démissionner.
This café needs to find another cook because this one just quit.

cuisinière f.   *cooktop, stove*
On doit remplacer notre vieille cuisinière des années 70.
We must replace our old cooktop from the '70s.

culotté(e) *cheeky, bold*
Il est tellement culotté qu'il ose dire des choses que personne d'autre ne dirait.
He's so cheeky that he dares say things that no one else would say.

D

d'abord *first*
D'abord on passe par la boulangerie et ensuite on ira chez le fleuriste.
First we are going to the bakery, and then we'll go to the flower shop.

dame f. *lady*
Mon poème préféré de Baudelaire est "À une dame créole".
My favorite Baudelaire poem is "To a Creole Lady."

danger m. *danger*
Le reportage estime que les sans-abris sont de plus en plus en danger de nos jours.
The report says that the homeless are more and more in danger these days.

dangereux(-euse) *dangerous*
Le hockey sur glace n'est pas aussi dangereux que le football américain.
Ice hockey isn't as dangerous as football.

dans *in*
J'ai mis la nouvelle sculpture dans le salon.
I put the new sculpture in the living room.

danser *to dance*
J'espère pouvoir danser ce soir au bal.
I hope I'm able to dance at the ball tonight.

date f. *date*
Quelle est la date aujourd'hui?
What's the date today?

de *of, from*
Elle prend le train de Nantes à Paris.
She's taking the train from Nantes to Paris.

déballer *to unpack*
On doit déballer nos valises avant l'arrivée de nos amis.
We have to unpack our suitcases before our friends arrive.

débarrasser, se … de   *to get rid off*
Elle doit se débarrasser de tous ses amis parasites.
She must get rid of all her parasitical friends.

débile   *stupid, idiotic*
Je trouve ce film vraiment débile.
I think this film is really idiotic.

déborder   *to overflow*
Arrête de verser de l'eau dans ce verre, il déborde!
Stop pouring water in this glass—it's overflowing!

débouché m.   *opening, outlet*
Il y a de nombreux debouchés dans le marché asiatique en ce moment.
There are many openings in the Asian market at this time.

debout   *standing up*
Il y avait tellement de spectateurs qu'on n'a pas pu trouver de
   place, on a du rester debout.
*There were so many spectators that we couldn't find a seat; we had to
   remaining standing.*

débrouiller, se   *to manage*
Elle se débrouille mal à cause de tous ses problèmes financiers.
She's managing poorly because of all her financial problems.

débutant(e)   *beginner*
C'est un cours pour débutants.
It's a course for beginners.

décalage horaire   *time difference, jet lag*
Comme ils souffrent du décalage horaire, ils ne vont pas pouvoir
   sortir avec nous ce soir.
*Since they're suffering from jet lag, they're not going to be able to go
   out with us tonight.*

déception f.   *disappointment*
Sa déception après la défaite était totale.
His disappointment after the defeat was complete.

déchets m. pl.   *trash, garbage*
On était déçus de voir tous ces déchets par terre au parc.
We were disappointed to see all this trash on the ground at the park.

déchiffrer   *to decipher, to decode*
J'ai du mal à déchiffrer son écriture.
I'm having a heard time deciphering her handwriting.

déchirant(e)   *heart-rending, agonizing*
La décision de déménager de leur maison est complètement
déchirante pour elles.
The decision to move from their house is completely agonizing for them.

décidément   *really*
Alors, décidément tu aimes le chocolat!
Wow, you really like chocolate!

décider   *to decide*
Rien n'est décidé pour le moment.
Nothing has been decided for the moment.

déclencher   *to spark, to cause, to start*
Les actions de la direction ont déclenché de nombreuses
manifestations.
The management's actions have set off numerous protests.

décontracté(e)   *relaxed*
Tu as l'air bien décontracté en ce moment.
You seem really relaxed these days.

décortiquer   *to shell; to analyze, to dissect*
Décortiquons ces noix pour notre salade.
Let's shell these nuts for our salad.
Notre prof de philo aime décortiquer nos arguments.
Our philosophy professor loves to dissect our arguments.

découler   *to follow from, to result from*
Cette idée découle de la logique perverse de ce parti politique.
This idea follows from the perverse logic of this political party.

découper   *to cut up, to carve*
Peux-tu découper le rôti de bœuf?
Can you carve the roast beef?

décourager   *to discourage, to dishearten*
Tu nous décourages avec tous tes commentaires négatifs.
You're discouraging us with all of your negative comments.

découragement m.   *discouragement*
Il est accablé par le découragement.
He is overcome by discouragement.

découvrir   *to discover*
Les scientifiques espèrent découvrir une cure contre le cancer.
Scientists hope to discover a cure for cancer.

déçu(e)   *disappointed*
Je suis déçu d'apprendre ces nouvelles.
I'm disappointed to learn of this news.

dedans   *inside*
J'aime bien cette tarte parce qu'il n'y a pas de sucre dedans.
I like this tart because there isn't any sugar in it.

défendre   *to forbid*
Son père lui a défendu de fumer dans la maison.
His father forbade him from smoking in the house.

défi m.   *challenge*
Refaire l'image de notre enterprise est un veritable défi.
Redoing our company's image is a true challenge.

déglinguer, se   *(colloquial) to break, to fall apart, to go bust*
Eh bien, tout ce que j'ai acheté dans ce magasin se déglingue!
Well, everything I bought from this store is falling apart.

dégoiser   *(colloquial) to prattle on about, to rattle on*
Mon mari ne cesse jamais de dégoiser, qu'est-ce qu'il m'embête!
My husband never stops rattling on; he annoys me so!

dégonfler, se   *to deflate; (colloquial) to chicken out*
Le pneu se dégonfle, quel emmerdement.
The tire is deflating. What a hassle.
Toi , tu te dégonfles toujours à la dernière minute!
You always chicken out at the last minute!

dégourdi(e)   *bright, sharp, shrewd*
Leurs fils n'est pas très intelligent mais il est dégourdi.
Their son isn't very intelligent but he is street-smart.

dégourdir   *to stretch; (colloquial) to teach someone a thing or two*
Les footballeurs se dégourdissent avant leur match.
The football players are stretching before their game.
Il t'a bien dégourdi, hein?
So, he really taught you a thing or two.

dégoût m.   *disgust*
Je ressens un sentiment de dégoût pour vos idées dangereuses.
I have a feeling of disgust for your dangerous ideas.

dégoûter   *to disgust, to make someone feel sick*
Les produits laitiers me dégoûtent, je ne peux pas les manger.
Dairy products disgust me; I can't eat them.

dégringoler   *to take a tumble, to tumble down*
J'ai vu mon chat sauter de l'étagère et puis j'ai vu tous mes livres dégringoler.
I saw my cat jump off the bookshelf and then I saw all my books tumble down.

déguerpir   *to clear away, to beat it (colloquial)*
On a vite déguerpi après l'arrivée soudaine des flics.
We beat it after the sudden arrival of the police.

dégueulasse   *(colloquial) disgusting, nasty, gross*
Christophe trompe sa femme depuis des années, tu sais. Oui, je sais. Je trouve ça déguelasse.
You know, Christophe has been cheating on his wife for years. Yeah, I know. I think it's disgusting.

dehors   *outside*
Allons dehors pour prendre l'air.
Let's go outside to get some air.

déjà   *already*
J'ai déjà vu tous les films de Cédric Klapisch.
I've already seen all of Cédric Klapisch's films.

déjeuner   *to have lunch*
Tu peux déjeuner avec moi demain?
Can you have lunch with me tomorrow?

délaisser   *to abandon, to neglect*
Comme la plupart de mes amis ne me téléphone plus, je me sens un peu délaissé.
Since most of my friends don't call me any more, I feel sort of neglected.

délecter, se   *to delight in doing something*
L'été on se délecte à dîner dehors.
In the summertime we delight in having dinner outside.

demain   *tomorrow*
Nous irons à Londres demain.
We will go to London tomorrow.

demander   *to ask*
Il nous demande de faire de notre mieux.
He's asking us to do our best.

démanger *to itch*
La piqûre d'abeille que j'ai chopée me démange.
The bee sting that I got itches me.

démarrer *to start*
Ma voiture ne veut pas démarrer ce matin.
My car won't start this morning.

déménager *to move house*
On déménage à la fin du mois.
We're moving at the end of the month.

démener, se *to thrash about or struggle; to exert oneself*
Notre commune se démène depuis quelques années pour trouver une solution à notre problème de déchets.
Our town has been struggling for several years to find a solution to our trash problem.

démettre *to dismiss*
Le patron dit qu'il va démettre tous les salariés si notre production n'augmente pas.
The boss says that he's going to dismiss all the employees if production doesn't increase.

demeurer *to stay, to remain*
Je demeure dans cette maison jusqu'à ce qu'il me dise de partir.
I'm remaining in this house until he tells me to leave.

demi *half*
C'est mon demi-frère.
He's my half-brother.

démodé(e) *out of style*
Ce pantalon est vraiment démodé, tu ne devrais pas le porter.
These pants are really out of style; you shouldn't wear them.

dent f. *tooth*
Il s'est cassé la dent en mangeant des noix.
He broke his tooth while eating nuts.

dentiste m. or f. *dentist*
Elle poursuit des études pour devenir dentiste.
She's studying to become a dentist.

départ m. *departure*
Téléphonez-nous avant votre départ.
Call us before your departure.

dépêcher, se   *to hurry*
Tu dois te dépêcher si tu ne veux pas manquer le train.
You should hurry if you don't want to miss your train.

dépendre de   *to depend on*
Tout cela dépend de ton effort personnel.
All of this depends on your personal effort.

dépenser   *to spend*
Quand on voyage on dépense énormément d'argent.
When you travel you spend enormous amounts of money.

depuis   *since, for how long*
Depuis combien de temps tu habites à Paris?
How long have you been living in Paris?

déranger   *to bother, to disturb*
Je ne veux pas te déranger maintenant.
I don't want to bother you now.

dernier(-ière)   *last*
Je l'ai vue la semaine dernière.
I saw her last week.

dérouler, se   *to happen*
Il va nous dire comment les choses vont se dérouler.
He's going to tell us how things are going to happen.

déroutant(e)   *puzzling*
Je trouve ces remarques déroutantes et peu utiles.
I find these remarks to be puzzling and of little value.

derrière   *behind*
Notre voiture est garée derrière le garage.
Our car is parked behind the garage.

des pl.   *some*
Ils veulent acheter des fleurs.
They want to buy some flowers.

dès   *from, as soon as*
Je vous contacterai dès mon retour.
I'll contact you as soon as I return.

descendre   *to come down, to go down*
Nous voulons descendre au prochain arrêt.
We want to get off at the next stop.

désirer   *to desire, to want*
Que désirez-vous?
What would you like?

désormais   *from now on, from then on*
Le corps du militaire repose désormais au cimetière familial.
*The body of the deceased military officer will be laid to rest from now on
    in the family cemetery.*

dessein, à m.   *on purpose, by design*
Il l'a fait à dessein.
He did it on purpose.

dessiner   *to draw, to design*
Les enfants dessinent des animaux avec des feutres.
The kids are drawing animals with markers.

destination f.   *destination*
On aimerait un vol à destination de Nice.
We'd like a flight to Nice.

destiné(e)   *destined for, bound*
Cette chanson est destinée à devenir un grand tube sur Internet.
This song is bound to become a big hit on the Internet.

désuet(-ète)   *old-fashioned, obsolete*
J'aime bien leur maison, elle a un charme désuet qui me plaît.
I like their house—it has an old-fashioned charm that pleases me.

détaler   *to bolt away, to take off*
Le moindre bruit fait détaler notre petit chat Minou.
The slightest noise makes our little cat, Minou, take off.

détester   *to loathe, to dislike*
Elle déteste le café, elle le trouve trop acide.
She dislikes coffee; she finds it too acidic.

détournement m.   *misappropriation, hijacking*
Il est accusé de détournement de fonds.
He's accused of misappropriation of funds.

détruire   *to destoy*
La bombe a détruit toute la ville.
The bomb destroyed the entire city.

dévaloriser   *to depreciate, to belittle*
Pourquoi tu me dévalorises devant tes amis?
Why do you belittle me in front of your friends?

devant   *in front of*
Attendons ici devant la porte.
Let's wait here in front of the door.

déveine f.   *(colloquial) bad luck, rotten luck*
J'ai vraiment la déveine, n'est-ce pas?
I've got really rotten luck, don't I?

développer   *to develop*
Georges veut développer un nouveau logiciel contre le plagiat.
George wants to develop a new software that catches plagiarism

devenir   *to become*
Juliette veut devenir pilote.
Juliet wants to become a pilot.

dévoiler   *to unveil, to reveal, to disclose*
Est-ce qu'on va dévoiler l'identité du criminel?
Is the identity of the criminal going to be revealed?

devoir m.   *duty, homework*
Ce salarié n'a aucun sens du devoir professionnel.
This employee has no sense of professional duty.

devoir   *to must, to have to*
Nous allons devoir passer à la pharmacie pour acheter mes
    médicaments.
We are going to have to stop by the pharmacy to buy my medication.

diable m.   *devil*
Ce gamin est un petit diable!
This kid is a little devil!

dieu m.   *God*
Les athées rejettent l'existence de Dieu.
Atheists reject the existence of God.

diffamer   *to defame, to slander*
Avec ces propos, vous risquez de diffamer votre ancien collègue.
With these words, you might be defaming your former colleague.

différence f.   *difference*
Quelle est la différence entre ces deux choses?
What's the difference between these two things?

difficile   *difficult*
Je trouve le calcul mental vraiment difficile.
I find mental arithmetic really difficult.

dîner *to have dinner*
On va dîner vers sept heures.
We're going to have dinner around seven.

dingue *crazy*
Ce que tu dis est complètement dingue!
What you're saying is completely crazy!

dire *to say*
Je n'ai rien à dire.
I don't have anything to say.

dire au revoir *to say good-bye.*
On doit vous dire au revoir maintenant.
We have to say good-bye now.

diriger *to direct, to lead, to be in charge of*
Il dirige cette enterprise et a donc beaucoup de responsabilités.
*He is in charge of this company so he has a lot of
    responsibilities.*

distance f. *distance*
Le sommet de la montagne est à une bonne distance d'ici.
The summit of the mountain is a good distance from here.

dizaine f. *dozen*
Le rédacteur en chef a reçu une dizaine de lettres au sujet de
    l'article diffamatoire que le journal a publié hier.
*The editor-in-chief has received a dozen letters about the slanderous
    article the paper published yesterday.*

doigt m. *finger*
Il s'est coupé le doigt en coupant une tomate.
He cut his finger while cutting a tomato.

dommage m. *shame, pity, damage*
C'est dommage que les enfants refusent de manger des épinards.
It's a shame that kids refuse to eat spinach.

dompter *to subdue, to tame*
Le dompteur n'arrive pas à dompter le tigre sauvage.
The trainer isn't able to tame the wild tiger.

donc *so, therefore*
Je pense, donc je suis.
I think, therefore I am.

donner   *to give*
J'espère que vous allez nous donner votre adresse.
I hope you're going to give us your address.

dorénavant   *from here on*
Dorénavant, la direction ne fera plus de photocopies pour les
    employés.
From here on, mangement will no longer make photocopies for employees.

dormir   *to sleep*
Ma mère prend des somnifères car elle a du mal à dormir.
My mom takes sleeping pills because she has a hard time sleeping.

douane f.   *customs*
Il faut passer par la douane si vous avez quelque chose à déclarer.
You need to go to customs if you have something to declare.

douche f.   *shower*
Je prends une douche avant de me coucher.
I'm taking a shower before going to bed.

douillet(-tte)   *cozy, soft, snug*
Je ne vais jamais enlever ce pull douillet!
I'm never taking off this cozy sweater.

douleur f.   *pain, cramp*
Il ne peut pas supporter la douleur de sa blessure.
He can't stand the pain from his injury.

douleureux(-euse)   *painful*
Il est en train de vivre une période douleureuse de sa vie: sa
    femme l'a quitté et ses enfants ne veulent plus lui parler.
*He's in the midst of a painful time in his life: his wife left him and his
    kids don't want to talk to him any more.*

doute m.   *doubt*
J'ai quelques doutes à cet égard.
I have some doubts where this is concerned.

douter de   *to have doubts about something*
Je doute de sa sincerité.
I have doubts about his sincerity.

doux (-ouce)   *soft, sweet*
Cette laine est vraiment douce.
This wool is so soft.

douzaine f.   *dozen*
Donnez-moi une douzaine d'œufs s'il vous plaît.
Please give me a dozen eggs.

drame m.   *drama*
J'aime les comédies mais je préfère les drames.
I like comedies but I prefer dramas.

drapeau m.   *flag*
Combien y a-t-il d'étoiles sur le drapeau chinois?
How many stars are on the Chinese flag?

drogue f.   *drug*
Elle a besoin de drogues—c'est une toxicomane.
She needs drugs—she's an addict.

droit m.   *right, law*
Vous n'avez pas le droit de me parler ainsi.
You don't have the right to talk to me like this.

droite f.   *right*
Le café où on a mangé hier est à droite.
The café where we ate yesterday is on the right.

dur(e)   *hard, difficult, harsh*
L'étudiant passe un examen très dur.
The student is taking a very difficult exam.

durcir   *to harden*
Notre gouvernement durcit sa politique en matière de pollution.
Our government is hardening its policy toward pollution.

durée f.   *length, duration, term*
Quelle est la durée de votre visite?
How long is your visit?

durer   *to last*
Combien de temps est-ce que le spectacle va durer?
How long is the show going to last?

E

eau f.   *water*
Je ne bois que de l'eau minérale plate.
I only drink flat mineral water.

ébauche f.   *preliminary draft, sketch*
L'architecte nous a montré l'ébauche de son projet.
The architect showed us the sketch of his project.

éblouir   *to dazzle, to stun*
Tu nous éblouis avec ton intelligence.
You dazzle us with your intelligence.

éblouissant(e)   *dazzling, stunning*
Selon Sylvie, le spectacle qu'ils ont vu hier soir était
    éblouissant.
According to Sylvie the show they saw last night was dazzling.

échanger   *to exchange*
Sophie passe par le magasin de chaussures pour échanger les
    sandales qu'elle a achetées l'autre jour.
*Sophie is stopping by the shoe store to exchange the sandals she bought
    the other day.*

échantillon m.   *sample*
J'aime cette marque parce qu'on reçoit toujours beaucoups
    d'échantillons avec chaque commande.
*I love this brand because you always receive lots of samples with each
    order.*

échéance f.   *due date, expiration date*
La banque nous a donné un avis d'échéance.
The bank sent us a due-date notice.

échec m.   *failure, setback, defeat*
Cela représente un grand échec pour notre enterprise.
This is a great setback for our company.

échouer   *to fail*
Tous les lycéens en terminale craignent d'échouer au bac.
*All students in the last year of high school are afraid of failing the bac-
    calaureate exam.*

éclater   *to burst, to explode, to break out*
La guerre civile de notre pays a éclaté il y a trois ans.
Civil war broke out in our country three years ago.

écœuré(e)   *nauseated, disgusted*
On est tous écœurés par votre conduite, Madame.
We are all disgusted by your behavior, Ma'am.

école f.   *school*
Il vient de trouver un poste dans une école près d'ici.
He just got a job at a nearby school.

écolo m. , f.   *(colloquial) "green," environmentally friendly, environmentalist*
Les écolos manifestent contre cette usine qui pollue nos fleuves.
The environmentalists are protesting against this factory that pollutes our rivers.

économe   *thrifty*
Si tu étais plus économe, tu n'aurais pas tous ces problèmes d'argent.
If you were more thrifty, you wouldn't have all of these money problems.

écouter   *to listen to*
Le soir nous aimons écouter du jazz à la radio.
At night we like to listen to jazz on the radio.

écran m.   *screen*
Ce téléviseur a un tout petit écran; je n'y vois rien!
This television has a really small screen—I can't see anything on it!

écraser   *to crush, to pound, to run over*
Je pense avoir écrasé un écureuil avec ma mobylette!
I think I ran over a squirrel with my moped!

écrire   *to write*
Si vous n'aimez pas cet article, vous devez écrire une lettre à la rédaction.
If you don't like this article, you should write a letter to the editor.

écriteau m.   *post, sign*
L'écriteau dit "Défense de Fumer", donc tu devrais éteindre ta cigarette.
The sign says "No Smoking," so you should put out your cigarette.

écrouler, s'   *to collapse*
Suite au séisme, plusieurs immeubles dans notre quartier se sont écroulés.
Following the earthquake, several apartment buildings in our neighborhood collapsed.

éculé(e)   *worn down, worn out, tired*
Ce journaliste nous fatigue avec ses expressions éculées.
This journalist is wearing us out with his tired expressions.

effacer *to erase*
Prends cette gomme et efface ce que tu as écrit.
Take this eraser and erase what you wrote.

effectuer *to carry out, to do, to complete*
Cette société est en train d'effectuer l'acquisition de cette petite
enterprise familiale.
This company is in the process of acquiring this small family-owned business.

effet m. *effect*
On sait très bien l'effet que cette loi va avoir sur les chômeurs.
*We know very well the effect that this law is going to have on the
unemployed.*

efficace *efficient, effective*
Cette technique n'est pas très efficace mais je l'aime bien tout de
même.
This technique isn't very efficient but I still like it.

effondré(e) *crushed, shattered*
Il est effondré par la mort de sa femme.
He is shattered by the death of his wife.

efforcer, s' *to strive, to try hard at*
Ces étudiants s'efforcent de réussir ce cours.
These students are trying hard to pass this course.

effort m. *effort*
Mais, fais un petit effort quand même!
But at least make an effort!

effrayer, s' *to be frightened*
Quand je suis chez moi tout seul parfois je suis effrayé.
When I am home alone I'm frightened sometimes.

effroyable *hideous, appalling*
Les conditions dans cette partie de la ville sont effroyables.
The conditions in this part of the city are appalling.

égal(e) *equal, the same*
Ça m'est égal.
It's all the same to me.

également *equally, likewise, also*
Si tu aimes la poésie de Verlaine, tu dois également lire les
poèmes de Rimbaud.
If you like Verlaine's poetry, you should also read Rimbaud's poems.

égalité f.   *equality*
La devise de la France est "Liberté, Égalité, Fraternité."
France's motto is "Liberty, Equality, Fraternity."

égard m.   *consideration, regard*
A cet égard, il est très compatissant.
In this regard, he is very compassionate.

égaré(e)   *stray, wild*
Quand on a vu ce chien égaré on a eu peur tout de suite.
When we saw this wild dog we instantly became afraid.

église f.   *church*
Ça fait trois ans que je n'ai pas mis les pieds dans une église.
It's been three years since I've set foot in a church.

elle f.   *she*
Elle est charmante, n'est-ce pas?
She's quite charming, isn't she?

emballer   *to wrap, to pack*
Je dois emballer ces papiers pour les emmener au centre de recyclage.
I should wrap these papers up and take them to the recycling center.

embassade f.   *embassy*
L'Ambassade américaine est juste en face de ce bâtiment.
The American embassy is just across the street from this building.

embaucher   *to hire*
Elle vient d'être embauchée par une banque internationale.
She was just hired by an international bank.

embêter   *to bother, annoy*
Ne les embête pas avec tes questions débiles!
Don't bother them with your stupid questions!

embouteillage m.   *traffic jam*
J'ai horreur de tous ces embouteillages, je préfère y aller à pied.
I hate all of these traffic jams. I prefer to go there on foot.

embrasser   *to kiss, to embrace*
J'ai envie de t'embrasser.
I feel like kissing you.

emploi m.   *job*
Si tu as besoin d'un emploi, cherche dans les petites annonces.
If you need a job, look in the want ads.

employé(e)   *employee*
Les employés de ce bureau sont tous nuls!
The employees in this office are all worthless!

encastrer   *to embed, to fit*
Dans leur nouvelle cuisine, tout est encastré: le four, le frigo, tout!
In their new kitchen, everything is built in—the oven, the fridge, everything!

enchanté(e)   *delighted, enchanted*
Je suis enchanté de faire votre connaissance.
I am delighted to meet you.

encore   *more, still*
Voulez-vous encore du pain?
Would you like more bread?

encre m.   *ink*
J'ai besoin d'acheter des cartouches d'encre pour mon stylo.
I need to buy some ink cartridges for my pen.

endroit m.   *place, spot*
Quel bel endroit!
What a beautiful spot!

enfant m.   *child*
Ce pauvre enfant n'a plus de famille, il est orphelin.
This poor child doesn't have any family; he's an orphan.

enlever   *to remove, to take away, to kidnap*
Si tu enlèves cette partie de l'essai, il sera plus facile à lire.
If you remove this part of the essay, it'll be easier to read.

ennui m.   *problem, boredom*
Je pense que tu vas avoir des ennuis avec ton coloc si tu ne paies pas les factures ce mois-ci.
I think your're going to have problems with your roommate if you don't pay the bills this month.

ennuyer   *to bother, to annoy*
Pourquoi tu veux m'ennuyer avec ce genre de question?
Why do you want to bother me with this type of question?

enseigner   *to teach*
Madame Garnier est capable d'enseigner le grec, le latin et l'italien.
Madame Garnier is able to teach Greek, Latin, and Italian.

ensemble   *together*
Allons ensemble au spectacle.
Let's go together to the show.

ensuite   *next, after, then*
D'abord nous avons vu un nouveau film qui vient de sortir et
ensuite nous avons pris un pot au bar.
*First we saw a new film that just came out, then we had a drink at
the bar.*

ensuqué(e)   *tired, beat, droopy*
On est tous ensuqués par ce travail infernal.
We are all tired from this hellish work.

entendre   *to hear*
Tu entends ce bruit à l'extérieur? Qu'est-ce que c'est?
Do you hear this noise outside? What is it?

entendu, bien   *of course*
Elle invitera toutes ses amies à la fête, bien entendu.
She will, of course, invite all of her friends to the party.

entre   *between*
Vous trouverez l'aire de jeux entre la librairie et le musée.
You'll find the playground between the bookstore and the museum.

entrée f.   *entrance, admission*
Où est la porte d'entrée?
Where is the entrance?

entrer   *to enter*
Elle est entrée par la porte de derrière.
She came in through the back door.

enveloppe f.   *envelope*
Tu peux me donner une enveloppe pour cette lettre?
Can you give me an envelope for this letter?

envelopper   *to envelop, to wrap*
Prends du papier pour envelopper ces déchets.
Take some paper to wrap up this trash.

envie f.   *desire*
Ce film me donne des envies de voyage.
This movie makes me want to travel.

envie de, avoir   *to feel like doing something*
Elle a envie de passer trois semaines au bord de la mer.
She feels like spending three weeks at the seaside.

envoyer   *to send*
Je dois acheter des timbres pour envoyer une lettre en Italie.
I need to buy stamps to send a letter to Italy.

épaule f.   *shoulder*
Il s'est fait mal à l'épaule.
He hurt his shoulder.

épicé(e)   *spicy*
La cuisine de ce pays est un peu trop épicée pour moi.
The food from this country is a bit too spicy for me.

équipe f.   *team*
Elle aime bien travailler en équipe.
She likes teamwork.

escale f.   *stopover*
Je préfère un vol sans escale, si possible.
I prefer a flight without stopovers, if possible.

escalier m.   *stairs*
J'ai peur des escaliers en colimaçon, je n'en prends jamais.
I am afraid of spiral staircases; I never take them.

espace m.   *space*
Il y a beaucoup d'espace dans cet apartment.
There is a lot of space in this apartment.

espagnol   *Spanish*
Elle parle espagnol couramment.
She speaks Spanish fluently.

espèce f.   *kind, species*
Il y a beaucoup d'espèces actuellement en voie de disparition.
There are many species that are becoming extinct right now.

espèces f.   *cash*
Ce restaurant n'accepte pas les cartes de crédit; il faut payer en
    espèces.
This restaurant does not accept credit cards; you must pay in cash.

espérer   *to hope*
Ils espèrent aller au Maroc cet été.
They hope to go to Morocco this summer.

espiègle   *impish, mischievous*
  J'adore les enfants de Maxine, ils sont tous tellement espiègles
    que l'on ne sait jamais ce qu'ils feront.
  I love Maxine's kids; they are all so mischievous that we never know
    what they'll do.

espion(-ne)   *spy*
  Elle est espionne. Elle travaille incognito.
  She's a spy. She works incognito.

esquisse f.   *sketch, outline*
  Fais une esquisse avant de commencer le tableau.
  Make a sketch before you start the painting.

essayer   *to try*
  Nous essayons de finir notre travail avant le début du match.
  We're trying to finish our work before the beginning of the game.

essence f.   *gasoline, petrol*
  L'essence coûte plus cher en France qu'aux Etats-Unis.
  Gasoline costs more in France than in the United States.

estomac m.   *stomach*
  Les filles ont trop mangé et maintentant elles ont mal à l'estomac.
  The girls ate too much and now have a stomachache.

et   *and*
  Caroline a acheté des carottes, des poivrons et de la salade au
    marché.
  Caroline bought carrots, peppers, and lettuce at the market.

étage m.   *floor*
  Notre appartement est au troisième étage.
  Our apartment is on the third floor.

état m.   *state*
  Le chef d'État est ici en visite officielle.
  The Head of State is here on an official visit.

États-Unis m. pl.   *the United States*
  Barack Obama est le quarante-quatrième président des États-Unis.
  Barack Obama is the fourty-fourth president of the United States.

éteindre   *to extinguish*
  Après quelques heures de lutte contre l'incendie, les pompiers
    ont pu réussir à l'éteindre.
  After several hours of fighting the fire, the firemen were able to put it out.

étoile f.   *star*
L'étoile du nord est très facile à repérer.
The North Star is very easy to find.

étourderie f.   *absent-mindedness, forgetfulness*
Il n'a pas fait cela par méchanceté mais plutôt par étourderie.
He didn't do that out of meanness, but rather out of absent-mindedness.

étrange   *strange, odd*
Je trouve ses propos étranges, et toi?
I find his words strange, do you?

étranger(-ère)   *foreigner, stranger*
Pour visiter notre pays, les étrangers auront désormais besoin d'un visa spécial.
In order to visit our country, foreigners will from now on need a special visa.

être   *to be*
Elle désire être psychiatre.
She would like to be a psychiatrist.

étroit(e)   *narrow, tight*
Malheureusement il a l'esprit un peu trop étroit pour accepter ces changements.
Unfortunately he's a little too narrow-minded to accept these changes.

étudiant(e) m. f.   *student*
Elle est étudiante à la fac.
She is a student at the university.

étudier   *to study*
Tu dois étudier sérieusement si tu veux réussir à l'examen.
You should study seriously if you want to pass the exam.

eux m.   *them*
Je pense à eux quand je visiste cet endroit.
I think about them when I visit this place.

évanouir, s'   *to faint, to pass out*
Comme il n'avait rien mangé avant la randonnée, il était sur le point de s'évanouir.
Because he hadn't eaten anything before the hike, he was about to pass out.

évantail m.   *fan*
Mon oncle collectionne les évantails chinois.
My uncle collects Chinese fans.

éveillé(e)   *alert*
On veut voir le nouveau-né quand il est bien éveillé.
We want to see the newborn when he is wide awake.

exagérer   *to exaggerate*
Le candidat exagère en disant que le gouvernement ne fait rien
    pour le peuple.
*The candidate exaggerates by saying that the government doesn't do
    anything for the people.*

examen m.   *exam, test*
Notre examen de physique était presque impossible!
Our physics test was practically impossible!

exaucer   *to grant, to fulfil*
La fée exauce les prières de la fille en lui donnant exactement ce
    qu'elle lui a demandé.
*The fairy answered the girl's prayers by giving her exactly what she
    wanted.*

excursion f.   *excursion, trip, outing*
Les écoliers attendent avec impatience leur excursion au zoo.
*The school children are impatiently waiting for their outing to
    the zoo.*

exemplaire m.   *sample, copy*
L'archéologue nous a dit que cet exemplaire-ci est très rare.
The archaeologist told us that this sample is very rare.

exemple m.   *example*
Le directeur de l'établissement leur donné beaucoup d'exemples
    du mauvais comportement de leur fille
*The school principal gave them many examples of the bad behavior of
    their daughter.*

exiger   *to require, to demand*
Le concierge exige que nous lui donnions les clés tout de suite.
*The building manager is requiring us to give her the keys
    immediately.*

expérience f.   *experience; experiment*
Je n'ai pas beaucoup d'expérience dans ce domaine.
I don't have a lot of experience in this area.
Les scientifiques montent une grande expérience au labo.
The scientists are starting a big experiment in this lab

expliquer   *to explain*
Tu devrais lui expliquer pourquoi tu ne veux plus le voir.
You should explain to him why you don't want to see him any more.

exprès   *on purpose, deliberately*
Tu l'as fait exprès!
You did it on purpose!

exprimer, s'   *to express oneself*
Elle s'exprime peu, elle est plutôt timide.
She doesn't express herself much; she's rather shy.

F

fabriquer   *to make*
Dans cette usine on fabrique des appareils photo numériques.
In this factory they make digital cameras.

fabuler   *to make up stories*
Quand ma fille était petite elle fabulait, elle avait une imagination
    incroyable!
*When my daughter was younger she made up stories; she had such an
    incredible imagination.*

face (en... de)   *in front of, across*
Mon bureau est en face du parc municipal.
My office is across from the municipal park.

fâcher   *to make someone angry*
J'ai des nouvelles qui vont te fâcher.
I have some news that is going to make you angry.

fâcher, se   *to become angry*
Ne dis pas cela à Margaux, elle se fâche facilement.
Don't tell that to Margot; she gets angry quite easily.

fâcheux(-euse)   *unfortunate, distressing*
L'aspect le plus fâcheux de ce malentendu est que tout le monde
    est perdant.
The most unfortunate aspect of this misunderstanding is that everyone loses.

facile   *easy*
L'interrogation était assez facile mais l'élève ne l'a a tout de
   même pas réussie.
The quiz was easy enough but the student still didn't pass it.

faciliter   *to facilitate, to make easier*
Le conseiller est ici pour faciliter leur transition à la maison de
   retraite.
*The counselor is here to ease their transition to the nursing
   home.*

facture f.   *bill, invoice*
Je viens de recevoir ma facture et on s'est trompé sur le montant
   à payer.
*I just received my invoice, and they made an error in the amount to be
   paid.*

faible   *weak*
Cet homme est trop faible.
This man is too weak.

faillite, faire f.   *to go bankrupt*
On vient d'annoncer que leur entreprise a fait faillite.
It was just announced that their business went bankrupt.

faim m.   *hunger*
Donne-lui à manger parce qu'il a faim.
Give him something to eat because he's hungry.

fainéant(e)   *lazy, idle*
Luc est un étudiant fainéant qui étudie très peu.
Luke is a lazy student who studies very little.

faire   *to do, to make*
Il songe à faire une tarte pour la fête ce soir.
He's thinking about making a pie for the party tonight.

fait, au   *by the way*
Au fait, je voulais te dire une chose.
By the way, I wanted to tell you something.

fait, en   *actually*
Ce sont des films qui sont en fait très mauvais.
These are movies that are actually quite bad.

falloir   *to be necessary*
Il faut se protéger du froid en hiver.
It is necessary to protect yourself from the cold in the winter.

falot(e)   *flat, colorless, pale*
Je trouve le héros de ce film un peu falot, et toi?
I think the hero in this movie is a bit flat, what do you think?

fameux(-euse)   *well-known, famous*
Balzac est le romancier le plus connu du début du 19ème.
Balzac is the most well-known writer of the beginning of the nineteenth century.

famille f.   *family*
Ma famille et moi pensons venir vous rendre visite.
My family and I are thinking about coming to visit you.

fané(e)   *whithered, faded*
Il n'y a rien de plus triste ques des fleurs fanées.
There's nothing sadder than faded flowers.

farfelu(e)   *(colloquial) eccentric, harebrained*
Encore une de tes idées farfelues? C'est pas possible!
Another one of your harebrained ideas? It's not possible!

fastueux(-euse)   *sumptuous*
Quel repas fastueux!
What a sumptuous meal!

fatigué(e)   *tired*
Cette nuit je n'ai pas fermé l'œil donc je suis fatigué ce matin.
Last night I didn't get a wink of sleep, so I am tired this morning.

fauché(e)   *(colloquial) broke*
Abdel est fauché, il n'a plus de fric.
Abdel is broke; he doesn't have any more money.

faufiler, se   *to sidle, to slip away*
Les gamins se sont faufilés avant qu'on les ait vus.
The kids slipped away before we saw them.

faut, il...que   *It is necessary that*
Il faut que ayons plus de patience avec elle, elle est très troublée.
It is necessary that we have more patience with her—she is quite troubled.

faute f.   *fault*
Ce n'est pas de ma faute!
It's not my fault!

feindre   *to feign*
Je suppose qu'elle va feindre d'être malade.
I suppose she's going to feign being sick.

félicitations f. pl.   *Congratulations*
Félicitations! On vient de voir les photos de ton nouveau-né.
Congratulations! We just saw the pictures of your newborn.

femme f.   *woman, wife*
La femme d'à côté est une musicienne très talentueuse.
The woman next door is a very talented musician.

fenêtre f.   *window*
On a besoin de remplacer les fenêtres pour que notre maison soit
    mieux isolée.
We need to replace our windows so that our house is better insulated.

fermé(e)   *closed*
La bibliothèque de notre village est fermée le weekend.
Our village's library is closed on weekends.

fermer   *to close*
Fermez la porte! Il y a des courants d'air.
Close the door! There's a draft.

fermeté f.   *firmness, confidence, resolve*
J'espère qu'ils garderont cette fermeté lors de leurs discours.
I hope they keep this resolve when they make their speech.

féru(e)   *to be interested in, keen on*
Elle est férue de mode depuis des années.
She's been interested in fashion for years.

fête f.   *party*
Je ne peux pas assister à la fête ce soir parce que j'ai trop de
    travail.
*I can't come to the party tonight because I have too much
    work.*

feu m.   *fire*
Le bâtiment abandonné a pris feu hier soir.
The abandoned building caught on fire last night.

feuillage m. *foliage*
Le feuillage de ces arbres est magnifique.
The foliage of these trees is magnificent.

feuille f. *leaf*
Il n'y a rien de plus joli que les feuilles qui tombent en automne.
There is nothing prettier than leaves falling in autumn.

feuilleter *to leaf through, to page through*
Elle aime feuilleter les magazines au lieu de les acheter.
She likes to leaf through magazines instead of buying them.

fiable *reliable, dependable*
Cette voiture est très fiable, elle démarre toujours.
This car is very reliable; it always starts.

fiancé(e) m. (pl.) *fiancé, betrothed*
Je viens de faire la connaissance de son charmant fiancé.
I just met her charming fiancé.

ficher *to give, to do*
Ça me fiche la migraine.
It's giving me a migraine.

ficher, s'en *to not give a damn*
Qu'il le fasse ou non, je m'en fiche.
Whether he does it or not, I don't give a damn.

fier à, se *to trust, to rely on*
Je me fie complètement à elle.
I trust her completely.

fièvre f. *fever*
Cet enfant a une fièvre élevée—emmenez-le à la salle des urgences.
This child has a high fever—take him to the emergency room.

figue f. *fig*
Au Maroc on a mangé des figues vraiment superbes.
We ate some really superb figs in Morocco.

figure f. *face*
Elle se lave la figure avant de se coucher.
She washes her face before going to bed.

fil, un coup de m. *phone call*
Passez-nous un coup de fil quand vous serez prête à partir.
Give us a phone call when you're ready to leave.

fille f.   *girl, daughter*
Après trois fils, ils sont très heureux d'avoir une fille.
After three sons, they are very happy to have a girl.

film m.   *film, movie*
Je viens de voir un film déprimant.
I just saw a depressing movie.

filmer   *to film, to shoot*
Chut! On est en train de filmer!
Shh! We're in the midst of filming!

fils m.   *son*
J'ai deux filles et un fils.
I have two daughters and a son.

fin f.   *end*
Quelle est la fin de l'histoire?
What's the end of the story?

finir   *to finish*
Je dois finir mon travail avant de sortir.
I have to finish my work before going out.

flairer   *to smell, to sense*
Mon chat peut toujours flairer le danger.
My cat can always sense danger.

flâner   *to stroll, to roam aimlessly*
Elle aime bien flâner dans les rues de notre ville.
She likes to stroll the streets of our city.

fléau m.   *scourge, plague*
On est hanté par ce fléau depuis longtemps.
We've been haunted by this scourge for a long time.

flemmard(e)   *lazybones*
Je suis assez flemmard en ce moment, je n'ai pas envie de travailler.
I'm such a lazybones, I don't feel like working.

flemme, avoir la f.   *to be indifferent*
Je n'ai pas rendu le livre à la bibliothèque, j'avais la flemme.
I didn't return the book to the library; I couldn't be bothered.

fleur f.   *flower*
Quelle est ta fleur préférée? Moi j'aime bien les tulipes.
What's your favorite flower? Personally, I like tulips.

fleuve m.   *river*
Le Nil est le plus long fleuve du monde.
The Nile is the longest river in the world.

flic m.   *(colloquial) cop*
Après quelques minutes, les flics sont finalement arrivés sur la
    scène de l'accident.
*After a few minutes, the cops finally arrived at the scene of the
    accident.*

flippant   *downer, depressing*
Je ne veux pas le voir, il est flippant.
I don't want to see him; he's depressing.

flotter   *to float, to flutter, to hang*
Il y a un air de doute qui flotte dans l'air.
There is a an air of doubt hanging in the air.

flou(e)   *blurred, hazy, vague*
Comme son argument est plutôt flou, j'ai du mal à comprendre
    ce qu'il veut dire.
*Since his argument is rather hazy, I'm having a hard time understand-
    ing what he means.*

foi f.   *faith*
Il est parfois difficile de garder la foi.
Sometimes it's hard to keep the faith.

foire f.   *fair, exhibition*
Les écoliers attendaient avec impatience le jour de la foire
    annuelle du livre.
*The schoolchildren waited impatiently for the day of the annual book
    fair.*

fois f.   *time, times*
Combien de fois as-tu visité Montréal?
How many times have you visited Montréal?

foison f.   *plenty of, abundance*
Il y a des oiseaux à foison dans ce pré.
There is an abundance of birds in this meadow.

foisonner   *to abound*
Après son explication floue, il faut admettre que les questions
    foisonnent.
After his vague explanation, we must admit that questions abound.

foncer   *(colloquial) to tear, to go for it, to get a move on*
On doit foncer pour y arriver à l'heure.
We have to get a move on so we can get there on time.

fonctionner   *to function, to work*
Cet appareil ne fonctionne plus.
This device doesn't work any more.

football m.   *soccer, football*
Le football est un sport mondial alors que le football américain
n'est apprécié qu'aux États-Unis.
*Soccer is a worldwide sport, whereas American football is liked only in
the United States.*

forcément   *necessarily, inevitably*
Ce qu'il dit n'est pas forcément vrai.
What he's saying isn't necessarily true.

forfait m.   *fixed-price, package deal*
Il vaut mieux acheter le forfait parce que tout est compris.
It's better to buy the package deal because everything is included.

forme f.   *figure, shape*
Après deux ans de yoga intensif, elles sont en très bonne
forme.
After two years of intensive yoga, they're in very good shape.

fort(e)   *strong*
Même s'il n'est pas très musclé il est tout de même très fort.
Even if he's not very muscular, he's still quite strong.

fou(-olle)   *crazy*
Voici une autre idée folle de notre patron!
And here's another one of our boss's crazy ideas!

foudre f.   *lightning*
Pendant l'orage notre maison a été frappée par la foudre.
During the storm our house was struck by lightning.

fouiller   *to search through, to rifle through*
J'ai l'impression que quelqu'un a fouillé dans mes affaires.
I feel like someone has been rifling through my things.

fourchette f.   *fork*
Mets la fourchette à côté de la cuillière.
Put the fork next to the spoon.

fourrer　　*to stuff, to fill; (colloquial) to put, to stick*
La pâtissière a fourré le gâteau avec de la crème.
The baker filled the cake with cream.
Fourre tes vêtements dans ce sac!
Put your clothes in this bag!

frais(-aîche)　　*cool, fresh*
Il fait frais ici le matin mais il commence à faire plus chaud vers midi.
It's cool here in the morning, but it starts to get warmer around noon.

français m.　　*French*
Je parle français et un peu espagnol aussi.
I speak French and a little Spanish, too.

Français(e) m. f.　　*French*
Il s'est marié avec une Française.
He married a Frenchwoman.

franchir　　*to cross, to get over, to overcome*
Les coureurs ont franchi la ligne d'arrivée tous ensemble.
The runners crossed the finish line all together.

francophone　　*French-speaking*
Voilà la première fois que je visite un pays francophone.
This is the first time I am visiting a French-speaking country.

franquette, à la bonne f.　　*(colloquial) informal, simple, without any fuss*
On a invité nos voisins pour un repas à la bonne franquette.
We invited our neighbors for an informal meal.

frapper　　*to hit, to knock*
Ecoute—j'entends quelqu'un frapper à la porte!
Listen—I hear someone knocking on the door!

friand(e)　　*fond of*
Ma mère est très friande de fromage anglais.
My mother is quite fond of English cheese.

fric m.　　*(colloquial) cash, money*
J'ai besoin de fric, je suis à sec.
I need cash—I'm broke.

frileux(-euse)　　*sensitive to the cold*
Il faut mettre le chauffage avant l'arrivée de Charlotte, elle est frileuse.
We'd better put the heat on before Charlotte arrives; she is sensitive to the cold.

frimer   *to show off, to be a poser*
Je ne peux pas la supporter, elle frime constamment.
I can't stand her, she's constantly showing off!

frimousse f.   *sweet little face*
Elle est à qui, cette petite frimousse sur la photo?
Whose sweet little face is that in the photo?

fringale, avoir la f.   *(colloquial) to have a raging hunger*
Il y a quelque chose à manger ici? J'ai la fringale.
Is there anything to eat here? I'm starving.

fringant(e)   *snappy, dashing*
On a rencontré un homme fringant ce soir au bal.
We met a dashing man this evening at the ball.

friqué(e)   *filthy rich*
Demande-lui de te prêter de l'argent, il est vachement friqué.
Ask him to lend you money; he's totally filthy rich!

frisé(e)   *curly*
Quels jolis cheveux frisés!
What beautiful curly hair!

frisson m.   *shiver, shudder, thrill*
C'est un film qui me donne des frissons, je l'adore!
This film gives me the shivers. I love it!

frites f. pl.   *French fries*
J'essaie de ne plus manger de frites, elles sont très mauvaises
   pour la santé.
I'm trying to no longer eat French fries as they are very bad for your health.

frivole   *frivolous, trivial*
Ne la dérange pas avec tes questions frivoles!
Don't bother her with your trivial questions.

froid(e)   *cold*
Il fait très froid à Montréal en hiver.
It's very cold in Montreal in the winter.

froissé(e)   *creased, crumpled; offended*
On a trouvé des tas de papiers froissés par terre dans le bureau
   du poète.
We found a ton of crumpled papers on the floor of the poet's office.
Excusez-moi, je ne voulais pas vous froisser.
Excuse me, I didn't mean to offend you.

frôler   *to brush up against, to skim*
Quand sa main a frôlé la mienne, j'ai éprouvé un grand frisson.
When her hand brushed up against mine, I felt a great thrill.

front m.   *forehead, front*
Les ouvriers veulent organiser un front politique.
The workers want to organize a political front.

frontière f.   *border*
La frontière entre la France et l'Italie est très facile à passer.
The border between France and Italy is very easy to cross.

frotter   *to rub, to scrub*
Tu dois frotter ces deux branches ensemble pour faire un feu.
You should rub these two sticks together to make a fire.

fugace   *transient, brief, fleeting*
Le plaisir de l'amour est parfois fugace et toujours difficile à décrire.
The pleasure of love is sometimes fleeting and always difficult to describe.

fuir   *to flee, to run away from, to avoid*
J'ai vu le collègue avec lequel je me suis disputé, mais il a fui.
I saw the colleague with whom I got into the argument, but he avoided me.

fulgurant(e)   *dazzling, brilliant*
Elle a une idée fulgurante.
She has a brilliant idea.

fumée f.   *smoke*
Il n'y a pas de fumée sans feu.
Where there's smoke there's fire.

fumer   *to smoke*
Il n'est pas facile pour mon père de cesser de fumer après trente ans.
It's not easy for my father to quit smoking after thirty years.

fuser   *to burst forth, to spurt*
Après la pluie diluvienne, l'eau fusait des égouts et les passants ont eu très peur.
After the torrential rains, water started bursting forth from the sewers and the passers-by became quite frightened.

futé(e)   *clever, sharp*
Il est très futé; il sait comment se débrouiller dans ce genre de situation.
He's very clever; he knows how to manage in this type of situation.

G

gâcher   *to ruin, to wreck*
Ne mets pas trop de sel dans la sauce, tu vas la gâcher!
Don't put too much salt in the sauce, you're going to ruin it!

gaffe f.   *blunder, mistake*
Elle a fait une grave gaffe.
She made a huge blunder.

gagner   *to win, to earn*
Elle gagne de l'argent en vendant des fleurs.
She earns money by selling flowers.

gai(e)   *happy, gay*
Quelle est cette chanson gaie que tu fredonnes?
What is this happy song you're humming?

gai   *gay, homosexual*
Didier lutte pour le mariage gai.
Didier is fighting for gay marriage.

galère f.   *(colloquial) galley, hell*
Je déteste ce travail, quelle galère!
I hate this job, what hell!

galérer   *(colloquial) to have a hard time, to slog*
Qu'est-ce qu'on galère avec ce projet. C'est un cauchemar!
Boy, are we having a hard time with this project. What a nightmare!

gamin(e) m. (f.)   *(colloquial) kid*
Ce gamin a perdu son chiot et le cherche partout.
This little kid lost his puppy and is looking for him everywhere.

gant m.   *glove*
Cela me va comme un gant.
It fits me like a glove.

garantir   *to guarantee*
Le vendeur garantit son produit à ses clients.
The merchant is guaranteeing his product to his customers.

garçon m.   *boy*
Ce jeune garçon est caractériel, il n'écoute jamais sa mère.
This young boy is a troublemaker; he never listens to his mother.

garde m.   *guard, watchmen*
Vite! La garde de nuit nous a vus!
Quick! The night watchman saw us!

gare f.   *train station*
Peut-on prendre un taxi pour aller à la gare?
Can we take a cab to go to the train station?

gare routière f.   *bus station*
La gare routière est à cinq minutes d'ici.
The bus station is five minutes from here.

garer   *to park*
J'ai horreur de garer cette grande voiture en ville.
I hate parking this big car in the city.

gaspiller   *to waste*
Tu gaspilles tout ton argent en achetant des trucs sans intérêt.
You waste all your money by buying stupid useless things.

gâter   *to spoil, to indulge*
C'est un père qui gâte trop ses enfants.
This father spoils his kids too much.

gauche   *left*
Dans certains pays, il ne faut jamais serrer la main avec la main gauche.
In some countries you should never shake with the left hand.

gazouiller   *to chirp, to babble*
J'aime écouter les oiseaux gazouiller dans le parc près de chez moi.
I like to listen to the birds chirping in the park close to my house.

geler   *to freeze*
Ce liquide ne gèle pas.
This liquid doesn't freeze.

gémir   · *to groan, to whimper*
Le petit chiot gémit tout le temps, il veut sortir.
The little puppy whimpers all the time; he wants to go outside.

gêner   *to bother, to embarrass*
Je ne veux pas vous gêner, mais il y a quelqu'un au téléphone qui
veut vous parler.
*I don't want to bother you, but there is someone on the phone who
wants to talk to you.*

généraliser, se   *to bring into general use, to generalize, widespread*
Cette méthodologie se généralise de plus en plus.
This methodology is becoming more and more widespread.

génial(e)   *great, brilliant*
Génial! On a trouvé notre chien qui s'était sauvé il y a trois jours.
Great! We found our dog that had run away three days ago.

genou(x) m. (pl.)   *knee(s)*
Suite à sa chute, l'athlète a mal aux genoux.
After his fall, the athlete's knees hurt.

genre m.   *sort, type, kind*
Quel genre de fromage aimes-tu?
What type of cheese do you like?

gens m. pl.   *people*
Il ne faut pas faire attention à ce que disent les gens que tu ne connais pas.
You shouldn't pay attention to what is said by people you don't know.

gentil(le)   *nice, kind*
Notre nouveau prof est intelligent mais pas très gentil.
Our new teacher is smart but not very nice.

gérant(e)   *manager*
Je vous présente la nouvelle gérante de nos affaires, Madame Lemtouni.
Let me intoduce you to our new business manager, Mrs. Lemtouni.

gérer   *to manage*
Il a mal géré ce projet.
He managed this project badly.

giboulée f.   *sudden downpour, cloudburst*
On faisait un pique-nique quand tout d'un coup une giboulée a commencé.
We were having a picnic when all of a sudden a downpour started.

gifle f.   *a slap in the face*
Il m'a flanqué une gifle.
He gave me a slap in the face.

gîte m. *shelter, rental cottage*
On a trouvé un gîte dans le Limousin pour un très bon prix sur Internet.
We found a rental cottage in the Limousin region for a really good price on the Internet.

givré(e) *(colloquial) bonkers, nuts, crazy*
Elle est complètement givrée, ta sœur!
Your sister is completely crazy!

glace f. *ice, ice cream, mirror*
Veux-tu de la glace au chocolat?
Would you like some chocolate ice cream?
On voit notre image dans la glace.
We can see our reflection in the mirror.

gober *to swallow hook, line, and sinker*
Ne me dis pas que tu as gobé tout ce qu'elle t'a dit!
Don't tell me your bought everything she said hook, line, and sinker!

godiche f. *awkward, oafish, silly*
Qu'est-ce qu'elle est godiche!
She's so awkward!

gonfler *to swell, to fill up, to blow up*
Tu devrais faire gonfler tes pneus avant de quitter la station service.
You should have your tires filled up before leaving the gas station.

gorge f. *throat*
J'ai mal à la gorge.
My throat hurts.

gosse m. or f. *kid*
Quel salle gosse!
What a bratty kid!

gourer, se *(colloquial) to goof, to mess up, to foul up*
Il s'est gouré et on doit tout refaire maintenant.
He messed up and now we need to do everything over.

goûter *to taste*
J'aime bien goûter tous ces fromages de votre région.
I really like tasting all these cheeses from your region.

goûter m.   *afternoon snack*
Mes enfants prennent du pain avec du fromage comme goûter.
My kids have bread with cheese for an afternoon snack.

goutte f.   *drop*
Donne-moi juste une goutte de vin, s'il te plaît.
Give me just a drop of wine, please.

gouvernement m.   *government*
Certains n'ont pas assez de respect pour notre
gouvernement.
Some people don't have enough respect for government.

grand(e)   *big, large*
Ce bateau a la plus grande voile que j'ai jamais vue.
This boat has the biggest sail I've ever seen.

grand magasin m.   *department store*
Au lieu d'acheter en ligne, je préfère fréquenter les grands
magasins.
Instead of shopping online I prefer going to department stores.

grandeur f.   *size, greatness*
L'univers est d'une grandeur inestimable.
The universe is of an inestimable size.

grandir   *to grow, to grow up*
Il a grandi dans la misère totale.
He grew up in total poverty.

gratter   *to scratch*
Je gratte cette piqûre de moustique.
I'm scratching this mosquito bite.

gré m.   *will*
Elle est allée voir le prof de son propre gré.
She went to see the professor of her own accord.

greffe f.   *graft, transplant*
Le vieil homme malade attend une greffe du cœur.
The ill elderly man is waiting for a heart transplant.

grève f.   *strike*
Les ouvriers menacent de faire la grève.
The workers are threatening to strike.

grignoter   *to nibble, to snack*
Il n'est pas bon de grignoter entre les repas.
It isn't good to snack between meals.

grimacer *to make a face, to grimace*
Le bébé grimace quand il entend le chien aboyer.
The baby makes a face when he hears the dog barking.

grimper *to climb*
Si on grimpe cette grande colline, on aura une très belle vue de la vallée.
If we climb this big hill, we'll have a really beautiful view of the valley.

grincheux (-euse) *cranky*
Je ne veux surtout pas parler à cette dame grincheuse aujourd'hui—elle m'énerve!
Above all I don't want to talk to that cranky woman today—she bugs me!

gris(e) *gray*
Tu es très beau dans ton costume gris; mets-le pour ton entretien d'embauche.
You are really handsome in your gray suit; wear it for your job interview.

grognon(-ne) *grouchy*
Attention, il est un peu grognon ce matin!
Watch out, he's a bit grouchy this morning!

gronder *to scold*
Je me suis fait gronder par le prof.
I got scolded by the professor.

gros(se) *fat*
Ce gros oiseau est si drôle!
This fat bird is so funny!

grossir *to put on weight, to get bigger*
Un sumo doit faire l'effort de constamment grossir.
A Sumo wrestler needs to make the effort to constantly gain weight.

groupe m. *group*
Un groupe d'ingénieurs vient en visite officielle demain.
A group of engineers is coming on an official visit tomorrow.

guérir *to heal, to recover*
Pour bien guérir de cette maladie, il faut prendre des antibiotiques.
To really recover from this illness, it's necessary to take antibiotics.

guerre f.   *war*
Ces deux pays sont constamment en guerre l'un avec l'autre.
These two countries are constantly at war with each other.

guetter   *to watch, to keep a look out for*
On guette l'arrivée du nouveau portable.
We're keeping a look out for the new cellphone.

guichet m.   *ticket office*
Elle nous a dit de récupérer nos billets au guichet.
She told us to pick up our tickets at the ticket office.

guide m.   *guide, guidebook*
Le guide nous a montré plein de sites intéressants.
The guide showed us many interesting sites.

H

habiller, s'   *to get dressed*
Je dois m'habiller pour aller à l fête.
I need to get dressed to go to the party.

habiter   *to live, to dwell*
Vincent habite dans la deuxième maison à gauche.
Vincent lives in the second house on the left.

habitude f.   *habit*
Elle a fait cela par habitude.
She did that out of habit.

habituer, s'   *to get used to*
Après deux semaines à Paris, Claire s'est habituée à la vie parisienne.
After two weeks in Paris, Claire got used to Parisian life.

haïr   *to hate*
J'ai ne comprends pas les gens qui haïssent les chats.
I don't understand people who hate cats.

hâler   *to tan*
J'ai le teint hâlé.
I've got a tan.

haletant(e)   *panting, breathless*
Me voilà haletant après seulement cinq minutes de jogging.
Here I am panting after only five minutes of jogging.

handicappé(e)   *handicapped*
Il n'y a aucun accès aux handicappés à ce bâtiment.
There is no handicapped access to this building.

hasard m.   *chance, coincidence*
J'ai trouvé ce nouveau disque de Phoenix par hasard.
I found this new album by Phoenix by chance.

hausser   *to raise*
Les deux ennemis haussent la voix en se parlant l'un à l'autre.
The two enemies raise their voices while speaking to each
    other.

haut(e)   *high, tall*
Ce bâtiment n'est pas très haut.
This building isn't very tall.

haut, en   *above, upstairs*
Notre chambre est en haut.
Our bedroom is upstairs.

heure f.   *hour, time*
Quelle heure est-il?
What time is it?

heureux(-euse)   *happy*
Elle très heureuse de pouvoir finalement visiter la Suède.
She's very happy to finally be able to visit Sweden.

hexagone f.   *hexagone, metropolitan France*
Avez-vous jamais visité l'Hexagone?
Have you ever visited France?

hier   *yesterday*
On est allé au café hier, mais c'était fermé.
We went to the café yesterday, but it was closed.

homme m.   *man*
Je trouve que l'homme là-bas ressemble beaucoup à mon frère.
I think that the man over there looks a lot like my brother.

homme/femme d'affaires   *businessman/woman*
J'ai remarqué que les hommes d'affaires sont tous très attachés à
    leur portable.
I've noticed that businessmen are all really attached to their
    cellphones.

honnête   *honest, decent*
Notre curé est un homme honnête.
Our priest is an honest man.

honte f.   *shame*
Tu devrais avoir honte de nous parler ainsi!
You should be ashamed to talk to us that way!

horaire m.   *timetable, schedule*
Il me faut un horaire récent.
I need a current timetable.

horreur f.   *horror, monstrosity*
Elle porte des sandales vertes avec des chaussettes jaunes?
   Quelle horreur!
She's wearing green sandals with yellow socks? What a monstrosity!

horripilant(e)   *exasperating*
On vient de passer une soirée horripilante avec notre voisin borné.
We just spent an exasperating evening with our narrow-minded neighbor.

hors (de)   *out, outside*
Ceci est hors de question!
This is out of the question!

hôtel m.   *hotel*
On a réservé une chambre dans un hôtel très chic.
We reserved a room in a really swanky hotel.

hôtel de ville m.   *city hall, town hall*
Ils vont se marier à l'Hôtel de Ville.
They're getting married at city hall.

houleux(-euse)   *stormy, turbulent*
La conversation est devenue houleuse quand j'ai mentionné
   l'argent qu'elle me devait.
The conversation became stormy when I mentioned the money she owed me.

humeur (f)   *mood*
Certaines personnes aiment siffler quand elles sont de bonne
   humeur.
Certain people like to whistle when they are in a good mood.

huppé(e)   *fancy, high-class*
Ils habitent un des quartiers huppés de notre ville.
They live in one of the high-class neighborhoods of our city.

hurler   *to yell*
L'entraîneur ne cesse jamais de hurler sur son équipe.
The coach never stops yelling at his team.

hurluberlu(e)   *oddball, crank*
Je dois admettre que mon oncle est un grand hurluberlu que j'ai
   du mal à comprendre.
*I must admit that my uncle is a huge oddball who I have a hard time
   understanding.*

I

ici   *here*
J'habite ici depuis 1975.
I've lived here since 1975.

idée (f)   *idea*
Quelle idée novatrice!
What an innovative idea!

il   *he*
Il est souvent drôle mais très sérieux aussi.
He's often funny but also very serious.

il y a   *there is, there are*
Il y a trop de monde ici.
There are too many people here.

illogique   *illogical*
Ce que vous dites est complètement illogique.
What you are saying is completely illogical.

illusoire   *illusory*
Notre progrès est illusoire.
Our progress is illusory.

illustre   *renowned, illustrious*
Hier soir on a fait la connaissance d'un des écrivains les plus
   illustres de nos jours.
Last night we met one of the most illustrious writers of our time.

ils(elles) m. (pl.)   *they*
Ils sont tellement inintelligibles que je comprends très peu de ce
   qu'ils disent.
They are so unintelligible that I understand very little of what they say.

imbiber   *to soak, to saturate*
Imbimber ce coton d'eau tiède et puis le mettre sur la blessure.
Soak this cotton in lukewarm water and then place it on the wound.

imbu(e), de sa personne   *full of oneself*
C'est un homme arrogant très imbu de sa personne.
He's an arrogant man who is quite full of himself.

immédiatement   *immediately*
Rendez-moi mon argent immédiatement.
Give me back my money immediately.

immeuble m.   *building*
Notre immeuble est très bien situé.
Our building has a great location.

immigré(e) m. (f.)   *immigrant*
Il y a beacoup d'immigrés qui sont récemment venus dans ce pays.
Many immigrants have recently come to this country.

immobile   *still, motionless*
Quand on a aperçu le python sur la terrasse, on est tous resté
    immobiles.
When we noticed the python on the terrace, we all remained still.

immobilier m.   *real estate*
Elle espère pouvoir trouver un emploi dans l'immoblier.
She hopes to find a job in real estate.

impeccable   *perfect, spotless*
Leur maison est toujours impeccable; tout est toujours rangé et bien
    nettoyé.
*Their house is always spotless; everything is always put away and
    spotless.*

imperméable m.   *raincoat*
Mets ton imperéeable parce qu'il va certainement pleuvoir ce matin.
Put your raincoat on because it'll certainly rain this morning.

implanter, s'   *to become established, to be built*
Cette usine s'est implantée dans notre region il y a dix ans.
This factory was built in our area ten years ago.

impoli(e)   *impolite*
Elle est si impolie que je refuse de l'inviter à notre fête.
She is so rude that I refuse to invite her to our party.

importer   *to import*
Le Mexique importe de plus en plus de produits d'autres pays
d'Amérique latine.
Mexico is importing more and more products from other Latin American countries.

impôt m.   *tax*
La société pour laquelle je travaille est obligée de payer plus
d'impôts cette année.
*The company that I work for is obligated to pay more taxes
this year.*

impuissant(e)   *powerless, helpless; impotent*
Je me sens impuissant face à mes peurs.
I feel powerless when faced with my fears.

incendie m.   *fire*
Il y a beaucoup d'incendies dans cette région aride.
There are many fires in this arid region.

incontournable   *incontrovertible, cannot be ignored*
Avant de prendre notre décision, il y a des faits incontournables
qui doivent être considérés.
*Before making our decision, there are incontrovertible facts that must be
considered.*

indigne   *disgraceful*
Vous n'allez pas tolérer son comportement indigne, j'espère.
I hope you're not going to tolerate his disgraceful behavior.

indiquer   *to point out, to indicate*
Tu peux m'indiquer le site dont tu me parlais?
Can you point out the website you were telling me about?

infirmier(-ière) m. (f.)   *nurse*
Les infirmiers de cet hôpital menacent de faire une grève si les
conditions de travail ne s'améliorent pas bientôt.
The nurses in this hospital are threatening to go on strike if work conditions don't improve soon.

information f.   *piece of information*
Ils ont une information qui risque de t'intéresser.
They have a piece of information that might interest you.

informatique f.   *computer science*
Je suis en informatique pour l'instant, mais je vais probablement changer de spécialisation.
I'm in computer science now but I'm probably going to change majors.

ingénieur(e) m. (f.)   *engineer*
Je suis un cours d'architecture parce que je veux devenir ingénieur civil.
I'm taking an architecture course because I want to become a civil engineer.

injuste   *unjust, unfair*
Cette décision me semble injuste.
This decision seems unjust to me.

inné(e)   *innate*
Certains talents semblent être innés.
Certain talents seem to be innate.

inopiné(e)   *unexpected, unforeseen*
Mes parents ont eu des problèmes inopinés donc ils ne nous rendront pas visite.
My parents had some unexpected problems so they won't be visiting us.

inouï(e)   *unprecedented, unheard of*
Elle a eu un succès inouï avec son premier roman.
She had an unprecedented success with her first novel.

inquiet(-ète)   *worried*
Comme on n' a pas de nouvelles, on est très inquiet.
As we haven't had any news, we're quite worried.

inquiéter, s'   *to worry*
Si les jeunes ne rentrent pas bientôt, je vais commencer à m'inquiéter.
If the young people don't come back soon I'm going to start to worry.

inquiétude f.   *worry, concerns*
Vos actions suscitent des inquiétudes parmi vos collègues.
Your actions are causing worries among your colleagues.

insinuer   *to insinuate, to imply*
Qu'est-ce que vous insinuez?
What are you implying?

insister *to insist*
Si la banque hésite à vous accorder un prêt, il faut insister.
If the bank hesitates to give you a loan, you must insist.

insolent(e) *insolent, impudent*
C'est un homme insolent.
He's an insolent man.

insolite *unusual, bizarre, out of the ordinary*
Cette photo est superbe; elle est vraiment insolite.
This photo is superb; it's really unusual.

installer *to put in, to install*
Le jeune couple a décidé d'installer une parabole sur
leur toit.
The young couple decided to install a satellite dish on their roof.

instar, à l' *following the example of*
A l'instar de son entraîneur, la jeune joueuse a gagné plusieurs
championnats.
*Following the example of her coach, the young player won several
championships.*

insu, à l' *without knowing*
Son mari a vendu leur voiture à son insu.
Her husband sold their car without her knowing about it.

interdit(e) *forbidden, off limits*
Cette boîte est interdite aux mineurs.
This nightclub is off limits to minors.

intéressant(e) *interesting; attractive*
C'est un philosophe qui a écrit beaucoup de livres intéressants.
He's a philosopher who has written many interesting books.
Le prix de cet appareil-photo est très intéressant.
The price of this camera is quite attractive.

intéresser *to interest*
Cet article risque de t'intéresser.
This article might interest you.

intérêt m. *interest*
Mon argent semble produire peu d'intérêt.
My money seems to earn little interest.

intérieur m.   *interior, inside*
Elles ont trouvé une jolie maison dont l'intérieur est complète-
    ment rénové.
They found a beautiful house with a completely remodeled
    interior.

intitulé(e)   *called, titled*
Elle a contribué à un livre intitulé "L'Histoire française".
She contributed to a book titled French History.

inutile   *useless, pointless*
Inutile de leur dire de nous téléphoner, ils ne le feront jamais.
It's pointless telling them to call us—they'll never do it.

investir   *to invest*
Notre pays investit beaucoup dans cette ville.
Our country is investing a lot in this city.

invisible   *invisible*
Ces mailles sont invisibles.
These stitches are invisible.

invité(e) m. f.   *guest*
Dépêche-toi parce que les invités arrivent dans trois quarts
    d'heure.
Hurry up because the guests are arriving in forty-five minutes.

inviter   *to invite*
Le couple a invité 150 personnes à son mariage.
The couple invited one hundred and fifty people to their wedding.

invraisemblable   *unlikely, implausible*
Je dois dire que votre explication est tout à fait invraisemblable.
I must say that your explanation is totally implausible.

ivre   *drunk*
Il doit être ivre après sept bières, non?
He must be drunk after seven beers, right?

ivresse f.   *intoxication, drunkenness; exhilaration*
Il faut éviter de conduire en état d'ivresse.
It's important to avoid driving while drunk.
C'est un poète dont les poèmes décrivent l'ivresse de l'amour.
This poet's poetry describes the exhilaration of love.

ivrogne m. f.　　*drunkard*
C'est un véritable ivrogne.
He's a real drunk.

J

jacasser　　*to chatter*
Elle déteste entendre ses élèves jacasser.
She hates hearing her students chatter.

jadis　　*in the past, in the old days*
Jadis les enfants aimaient bien ce jeu.
In the past children liked this game.

jalonner　　*to mark; to line*
Notre visite a été jalonnée de plusieurs événements désagréables.
Our visit was marked by several unpleasant incidents.
De jolis arbres jalonnent la route. C'est magnifique.
Some beautiful trees line the road. It's gorgeous.

jalousie f.　　*jealousy*
Elle est complètement tourmentée par la jalousie.
She is completely tormented by jealousy.

jaloux(-ouse)　　*jealous*
Clarice est devenue tout de suite jalouse quand elle a appris que
quelqu'un d'autre avait gagné la récompense.
*Clarice immediately became jealous when she learned that someone else
had won the award.*

jamais　　*ever*
As-tu jamais visité Nantes? C'est une ville extraordinaire.
Have you ever visited Nantes? It's an extraordinary city.

jamais, ne　　*never*
Je ne mange jamais de viande parce que je suis végétalien.
I never eat meat because I'm vegan.

jambe f.　　*leg*
Elle est tombée dans l'escalier et s'est fait mal à la jambe.
She fell on the stairs and hurt her leg.

jardin m.　　*garden*
Cet été-là on a passé énormément de temps ensemble dans son
jardin.
That summer we spent an enormous amount of time together in her garden.

jaune   *yellow*
Celui qui gagne l'étape du jour du Tour de France a le droit de porter le maillot jaune.
Whoever wins the day's stage of the Tour de France has the right to wear the yellow jersey.

je   *I*
Je suis ravi de faire votre connaissance.
I'm thrilled to meet you.

jetable   *disposable*
Ce stylo à encre est jetable? C'est incroyable!
This fountain pen is disposable? That's incredible!

jeter   *to throw, to throw out*
Il faut jeter les déchets dans la poubelle.
Throw the trash in the garbage can.

jeu m.   *game, match*
Eh bien, il faut jouer le jeu si tu veux réussir.
Well, you have to play the game if you want to get ahead.

jeune   *young*
Bonjour, jeune homme!
Hello, young man!

jeûner   *to fast*
Les Musulmans du monde entier jeûnent pendant le mois de Ramadan.
Muslims all over the world fast during the month of Ramadan.

jeunesse f.   *youth*
La jeunesse de nos jours s'intéresse beaucoup à l'environnement.
The youth of today is very interested in the environment.

joie f.   *joy*
Quelle joie de te revoir après toutes ces années!
What a joy to see you again after all these years!

joindre   *to connect*
Il est bon de joindre l'utile à l'agréable.
It is good to connect the useful with the pleasant.

joindre, se   *to join*
Je me joins à mes amis pour faire un piquenique.
I'm joining my friends for a picnic.

joli(e)   *pretty*

Il nous a offert un joli petit cadeau.
They gave us a lovely little present.

jonché(e)   *strewn, covered*

Malheureusement notre petit parc était jonché de déchets.
Unfortunately, our little park was covered in litter.

jouer   *to play*

Tu joues de la guitare? Moi aussi!
You play the guitar? Me, too!

jouet m.   *toy*

Il y a trop de jouets par terre dans ta chambre!
There are too many toys on the floor in your room!

jour m.   *day*

Nos invités seront là dans trois jours.
Our guests will be here in three days.

journal m.   *newspaper*

De plus en plus de gens lisent le journal sur Internet.
More and more people are reading the news on the Internet.

journalier (-ière)   *daily*

Je ne consomme pas l'apport journalier recommandé de fer donc
je dois manger plus d'épinards.
*I don't get the recommended daily amount of iron, so I should eat more
spinach.*

journée f.   *day*

On a passé une journée très agréable au bord de la mer.
We spent a really nice day by the seaside.

jucher   *to perch*

Un petit oiseau bleu est juché sur cette branche chaque matin.
A little bluebird perches on this branch every morning.

juge m.   *judge*

Le juge refuse de juger le fugitif en son absence.
*The judge refuses to hand down a sentence as long as the fugitive is not
present.*

juger   *to judge*

On a du mal à juger la situation.
We're having a hard time judging the situation.

jupe f.   *skirt*
Ma fille a acheté cette jupe à Paris l'été dernier.
My daughter bought this skirt in Paris last summer.

jurer   *to swear*
Je te jure que je ne lui ai rien dit.
I swear that I didn't tell him anything.

jusqu'à   *until, up to*
On sera à Bordeaux jusqu'à la fin du mois.
We'll be in Bordeaux until the end of the month

juste   *just, right, fair*
C'est un homme juste qui traite tout le monde avec respect.
He's a fair man who treats everyone with respect.

justement   *precisely, as it happens*
Je dois justement acheter des fleurs, donc je t'accompagnerai
   en ville.
As it happens, I need to buy flowers, so I'll go with you into town.

K

kermesse f.   *fair, festival (N. France and Belgium)*
Le village près de Caen tient une kermesse chaque printemps.
The village near Caen has a fair every spring.

kif-kif   *(colloquial) all the same*
Tu préfères du soda ou du citron pressé? Kif-kif! J'aime bien les deux.
Do you prefer soda or lemonade? It's all the same to me! I like both of them.

kilo(gramme) m.   *kilogram*
Je voudrais deux kilos de tomates, s'il vous plaît.
I'd like two kilos of tomatoes, please.

kilomètre m.   *kilometer*
Notre maison est à quinze kilomètres d'ici.
Our house is fifteen kilometers from here.

klaxonner   *to honk the horn*
Il est interdit de klaxonner dans certaines villes.
It is forbidden to honk the horn in certain cities.

krach m.   *crash*
Les marchés sont toujours bouleversés par le krach de 2009.
The markets are still shaken by the crash of 2009.

L

la   *the, it, her*
La maison n'est pas loin d'ici.
The house isn't far from here.
La pomme? Je vais la manger.
The apple? I'm going to eat it.
On la connaît, elle est très drôle.
We know her; she's very funny.

là   *here, there*
Anne, t'es où? Je suis là!
Anne, where are you? I'm here!

lac m.   *lake*
Cet été on va faire du canotage sur le lac.
This summer we're going to go canoeing at the lake.

lâcher   *to drop, to let go of*
Lâche-moi! Tu me fais mal!
Let go of me! You're hurting me!

lacune f.   *a gap, hole*
Malheureusement, il y a pas mal de lacunes dans votre argument.
Unfortunately, there are more than a few gaps in your argument.

laid(e)   *ugly*
Moi je trouve cette robe vraiment laide.
Personally I think this dress is really ugly.

laine f.   *wool, yarn*
Ma sœur me tricote un cardigan en laine.
My sister is knitting me a wool cardigan.

laisser   *to leave*
Je veux passer par la maison pour y laisser mes affaires.
I want to stop by the house and leave my things there.

lampe f.   *lamp*
Tu devrais remplacer cette lampe. Elle ne marche plus!
You should replace this lamp. It doesn't work any more!

lancer   *to throw, to launch, to hurl*
Il m'a lancé la balle mais je l'ai lâchée. Je suis nul en baseball!
He threw me the ball but I dropped it. I'm terrible at baseball!

langue f. *language, tongue*
Quelle est ta langue maternelle?
What is your native language?
Elle s'est brûlé la langue en buvant du thé chaud.
She burnt her tongue drinking hot tea.

laquelle(lesquelles) f. pl. *which one(s)*
Laquelle tu préfères—la verte ou l'orange?
Which one do you prefer—the green one or the orange one?

lard m. *bacon*
Je prends des œufs au lard, et toi?
I'm having eggs and bacon, and you?

large *broad, wide*
Au sens large du terme, on dirait qu'elle est libérale.
In the broadest sense of the term, you could say that she is liberal.

larguer *(colloquial) to dump someone*
Il a largué sa copine par texto. Quel con!
He dumped his girlfriend via a text message. What a jerk!

larme f. *tear*
Larmes aux yeux, l'enfant a rendu le petit chatton qu'elle avait
   trouvé à son voisin.
*Tears in her eyes, the child gave the kitten she'd found back to her
   neighbor.*

larmoyer *to whine*
Arrête de larmoyer ou je ne t'emmène pas au centre-commercial!
Stop whining or I won't take you to the mall!

lasser *to weary, to bore*
Claude nous lasse avec les histoires débiles de ses poissons
   rouges.
Claude is boring us with stories of his goldfish.

lavabo m. *washbasin, sink*
Elle a de la chance parce qu'elle a un lavabo dans sa chambre.
She's lucky because she has a sink in her room.

laver *to wash*
J'espère qu'ils vont laver leur voiture avant de partir en vacances.
I hope they're going to wash their car before going away on vacation.

laver, se *to wash oneself*
Le gamin doit se laver avant de se coucher.
The child needs to wash before going to bed.

le *the, it, him*
Je prends le métro pour aller à mon bureau.
I take the metro to go to work.
Mon manuel de physique? Je ne le veux plus. Vends-le!
My physics textbook? I don't want it any more. Sell it!
Je vais le voir demain.
I'm going to see him tomorrow.

leçon f. *lesson*
Le prof n'a rien préparé pour la leçon d'aujourd'hui.
The teacher didn't prepare anything for today's lesson.

lecteur DVD m. *dvd player*
Elle ne peut pas regarder ce film parce que notre lecteur DVD est
    en panne.
She can't watch the film because our dvd player is broken.

léger(-ère) *light*
Comme tu n'as pas très faim, tu devrais prendre un repas
    plutôt léger.
Since you're not very hungry, you should have a rather light meal.

lentement *slowly*
Conduis plus lentement, s'il te plaît!
Drive more slowly, please.

lequel(lesquels) m. pl. *which one(s)*
J'aime bien ce pantalon. Lequel?
I really like this pair of pants. Which one?

les *the, them*
Les chats sont aussi intelligents que les chiens. Moi, je les déteste tous.
Cats are as smart as dogs. I hate them all.

léser *to damage, to wrong someone, to injure*
Le juge trouve que personne n'a été lésé par les actions de l'accusé.
The judge believes that no one was injured by the actions of the accused.

lésiner *to skimp*
Elle ne lésine pas sur les produits de luxe!
She doesn't skimp on luxury products!

lettre f.   *letter*
Il a reçu une lettre qui l'a complètement bouleversé.
He received a letter that has completely upset him.

leur   *their, to them*
Vous avez leur argent?
Do you have their money?
Je leur ai parlé hier.
I spoke to them yesterday

leurre m.   *illusion, lure, decoy*
On croyait qu'ils avaient changé mais ce n'était qu'un leurre.
We thought they'd changed, but it was nothing but an illusion.

lever   *to raise*
Levez la main si vous voulez parler.
Raise your hand if you wish to speak.

lever, se   *to get up*
Je me couche tôt parce que demain je dois me lever à 6h.
*I'm going to bed early because tomorrow I have to get up at
   6 a.m.*

lèvre f.   *lip*
Elle a de jolies lèvres, non?
She has beautiful lips, right?

libre   *free, available*
Cette place est libre?
Is this seat free?

licencier   *to fire*
Après ses remarques désobligeantes, l'employé a été licencié.
After his insubordinate remarks, the employee was fired.

lieu m.   *place*
Ils ont choisi un lieu inoubliable pour leur mariage.
They've chosen an unforgettable place for their marriage.

ligne f.   *line*
Prenez la ligne orange pour aller au centre-ville.
Take the orange line to go downtown.

limite f.   *limitation, edge, boundary*
Tu ne connais pas tes propres limites.
You don't know your own limitations.

limiter   *to limit, to restrict*
Dorénavant on espère limiter ce genre d'activité.
From now on we hope to restrict this type of activity.

lire   *to read*
Il se plaint parce qu'il n'a pas assez de temps pour lire ce qu'il veut.
He's complaining because he doesn't have enough time to read what he wants.

liste f.   *list*
Faisons une liste de ce qu'on doit acheter au marché.
Let's make a list of what we need to buy at the market.

lit m.   *bed*
On vient d'acheter un lit pour notre fils.
We just bought a bed for our son.

litre m.   *liter*
Donnez-moi un litre de cidre, s'il vous plaît.
Give me a liter of cider, please.

livre m.   *book*
Les jeunes d'aujourd'hui achètent peu de livres.
Today's youth buy few books.

livrer   *to deliver*
Ce magasin de meubles refuse de livrer.
This furniture store refuses to do home delivery.

location f.   *renting out, rental*
On cherche une agence de location.
We're looking for a rental agency.

logiciel m.   *software*
Mon frère a développé un logiciel qui fait du traitement de texte.
My brother developed a software program that does word processing.

logique   *logical*
Votre question n'est pas logique.
Your question isn't logical.

loi f.   *law*
Le sénateur dit qu'il va voter contre cette loi ridicule.
The senator says that he'll vote against this absurd law.

loin   *far*
Notre voiture est garée un peu loin d'ici.
Our car is parked a bit far from here.

lointain   *distant, remote*
Elle vient d'un village bien lointain.
She comes from a very remote village.

loisir   *leisure, free time*
Vous pouvez nous répondre à votre loisir.
You can answer us at your leisure.

long(ue)   *long*
Ils ont joué un match bien long—presque trois heures!
They played a really long game—almost three hours!

louer   *to rent*
On aimerait bien louer un appartement dans le centre-ville, mais les loyers sont trop chers.
We'd like to rent an apartment downtown, but the rents are too expensive.

loufoque   *(colloquial) crazy*
Quelle idée loufoque! Je ne sais même pas quoi dire!
What a crazy idea! I don't even know what to say!

louper   *to miss; (colloquial) to flunk*
On a loupé notre train donc on attend le prochain.
We missed our train so we're waiting for the next one.
Elle a loupé son examen de biologie.
She flunked her bio test.

lourd(e)   *heavy*
Cette valise est trop lourde pour moi.
This suitcase is too heavy for me.

ludique   *playful*
Au début je croyais que ce roman était ennuyeux mais maintenant je trouve qu'il est assez ludique.
At first I thought this novel was boring, but now I think it's rather playful.

lugubre   *gloomy, mournful*
Il est toujours d'une humeur lugubre.
He's always in a gloomy mood.

lui   *him, him/her*
C'est qui? C'est lui.
Who is it? It's he.
Je lui parle au téléphone au moins trois fois par jour.
I talk to him/her at least three times a day.

lumière f.   *light*
Quand nous étions jeunes, mon frère avait une lumière
    stroboscopique dans sa chambre.
When we were young, my brother had a strobe light in his room.

lunatique   *moody*
Elle change d'humeur à tout instant, elle est assez lunatique
    en fait.
She's constantly changing her mood; in fact she's quite moody.

lune f.   *moon*
J'aime contempler la lune.
I love to contemplate the moon.

lunettes f. pl.   *eyeglasses*
Je ne peux rien voir sans mes lunettes.
I can't see anything without my glasses.

lutte f.   *struggle*
La lutte pour la liberté des femmes est très importante.
The struggle for women's rights is very important.

lutter   *to struggle*
Mon père est très engagé; il est constamment en train de lutter
    contre l'injustice.
My father is very committed; he's constantly struggling against injustice.

luxe m.   *luxury*
C'est quelqu'un qui a passé sa vie dans le luxe et n'accepte pas sa
    situation actuelle.
*He's someone who spent his life in luxury and can't accept his current
    situation.*

M

maculer   *to stain, to smudge*
Après avoir pleuré pendant une heure, son visage est maculé de
    mascara.
After she's cried for an hour, her face is mascara-stained.

madame f.   *Mrs., lady*
Madame Meunier travaille ici depuis vingt ans.
Mrs. Meunier has worked here for thirty years.

mademoiselle f.   *Miss*
Mademoiselle, je peux vous aider?
Miss, may I help you?

magasin m.   *store, shop*
Il y a plein de magasins dans ce quartier.
There are many stores in this neighborhood.

magique   *magical*
On a passé une soirée magique à Vaux-le-Vicomte.
We spent a magical evening at Vaux-le-Vicomte.

magouille f.   *skullduggery, scheming*
Ce ministre est bien connu pour ses magouilles politiques.
This minister is well-known for his political skullduggery.

main f.   *hand*
Il s'est brûlé la main en versant du café.
He burned his hand pouring coffee.

maintenant   *now*
Maintenant il y a très peu d'étudiants qui n'ont pas d'ordinateur.
Now there are very few students who don't have a computer.

maire m.   *mayor*
Cet homme brillant vient d'être élu maire de notre ville.
This brilliant man was just elected mayor of our town.

mairie f.   *town hall*
Ils se sont d'abord mariés à la mairie et puis à l'église.
They got married first at the town hall and then at church.

mais   *but*
J'aimerais faire une tarte Tatin mais je n'ai pas de pommes.
I'd like to make a Tatin tart but I don't have any apples.

maison f.   *house*
Ils sont en train d'acheter leur première maison.
They are in the process of buying their first house.

maître(-esse) m. (f.)   *elementary school teacher, owner*
Le maître essaie de calmer ses élèves avant l'épreuve.
The teacher is trying to calm his student before the test.
Qui est le maître de ce chien perdu?
Who is the owner of this lost dog?

maîtriser   *to get control of, to master*
Tu dois maîtriser ta colère avant de parler à ton patron.
You need to get control of your anger before talking to your boss.

mal   *badly*
Elle danse bien mais chante très mal.
She dances well but sings very badly.

mal, avoir   *to hurt*
Le gamin a mal aux bras après son difficile match de tennis.
The child's arms hurt after his difficult tennis match.

mal-bouffe f.   *(colloquial) junk food*
La mal-bouffe doit être éliminée de nos écoles.
Junk food should be eliminated from our schools.

malade   *sick*
Comme elle est malade, elle ne peut pas voyager.
Since she's sick she can't travel.

malentendu m.   *misunderstanding*
Rien n'est pareil entre eux depuis le grand malentendu de l'été
   dernier.
Nothing is the same between them since the big misunderstanding of last
   summer.

malgré   *in spite of, despite*
Malgré tous nos problèmes de transport, nos vacances étaient
   magnifiques.
In spite of all our transportation problems, our vacation was fantastic.

malheur m.   *misfortune, adversity, tragedy*
J'ai le malheur de vous dire que votre cours est annulé.
I have the misfortune of telling you that your class is canceled.

malice m.   *mischief, malice*
C'est un homme plein de malice qui aime faire souffrir les
   autres.
He's a man who is full of malice and likes to make others suffer.

malicieux(-euse)   *mischievous*
Cet enfant malicieux est très drôle, mais il cause des problèmes à
   l'école.
This mischievous child is very funny, but he causes problems at school.

malin(e) *clever, malicious, naughty*
Ce type malin fait toujours payer les autres.
This clever guy always gets other people to pay for him.

malingre *sickly*
C'est triste de voir que leur fils est si malingre.
It's sad to see that their son is so sickly

malintentionné(e) *malicious, ill-intentioned*
Encore une fois je suis hanté par des rumeurs malintentionnées.
Once again I am haunted by malicious rumors.

manger *to eat*
On va manger vers midi.
We're going to eat around noon.

manière f. *manner, way*
La manière dont vous me parlez est inacceptable.
The way in which you're speaking to me is unacceptable.

manifestation f. *demonstration, protest*
J'ai assisté à beaucoup de manifestations quand j'étais enfant, mes parents étaient babas!
I went to many demonstrations as a child—my parents were hippies!

manifestement *clearly, obviously*
Je ne vois pas du tout pourquoi tu dis ça; c'est manifestement faux.
I don't know why you're saying that; it's obviously false.

manigancer *to be up to something*
Alors, ça se voit que tu manigances quelque chose....
So, obviously you're up to something....

manipuler *to manipulate*
Elle manipule les résultats pour arriver à ses fins.
She manipulates the results in order to achieve her ends.

manquer *to miss, to lose*
Tu me manques.
I miss you.
On vient de manquer le train du 14h45.
We just missed the 2:45 train.

manteau m. *coat*
Mets ton manteau parce qu'il va faire très frais ce matin.
Put on your coat because it's going to be chilly this morning.

marché m. *market, open-air market*
Elle est passée par le marché en plein air pour acheter des fruits.
She stopped by the open-air market to buy some fruit.

marcher *to walk*
Après son accident, il a du mal à marcher.
After his accident, he has a hard time walking.

mari m. *husband*
Son mari est assez désagréable.
Her husband is somewhat disagreeable.

mariage m. *marriage*
Cet enfant est né du premier mariage de mon frère.
This child is from my brother's first marriage.

marier, se *to get married*
Malgré les protestations de ses parents, le jeune couple s'est
    marié à Las Vegas.
*Despite the protests from their parents, the young couple got married in
    Las Vegas.*

marron *brown*
Elle a des yeux marron.
She has brown eyes.

massif(-ive) *massive, huge*
Les géologues ont trouvé un rocher massif lors de leur fouille.
The geologists discovered a massive rock while on their dig.

massivement *overwhelmingly, massively*
Les actionnaires ont voté massivement pour une plus grande
    transparence dans les affaires de cette entreprise.
*The stockholders voted overwhelmingly for greater transparency in the
    affairs of this company.*

mastiquer *to chew*
Ce bébé est trop petit pour mastiquer sa nourriturre; il faut la
    couper en plus petits morceaux.
*This baby is too small to chew his food; you have to cut it up in smaller
    pieces.*

match m. *game, match*
On a vu un superbe match de tennis hier.
We saw a superb tennis match yesterday.

maudit(e)   *damned, blasted, cursed*
Je vais jeter ce maudit ordinateur par la fenêtre, j'en ai marre!
I'm going to throw this blasted computer out the window—I've had it!

maussade   *sullen, dull, bleak*
Ce paysage maussade me déprime.
This bleak landscape depresses me.

mauvais(e)   *bad, wrong*
Quelle mauvaise idée!
What a bad idea!
On a pris le mauvais chemin.
We took the wrong way.

me   *me, to me*
Il va me donner les clés.
He's going to give me the keys.
Elle me regarde.
She's looking at me.

mec m.   *guy (colloquial)*
J'ai vu le mec dont tu parlais l'autre jour.
I saw the guy you were talking about the other day.

médecin m.   *doctor*
Je dois voir le médecin car je me sens très malade.
I need to see the doctor because I feel really sick.

médias m. pl.   *the media*
La représentation de ce problème dans les médias est assez négative.
The representation of this problem in the media is somewhat negative.

médicament m.   *medication*
Elle a besoin de ce médicament pour combattre son infection.
She needs this medication to fight her infection.

méfiance f.   *mistrust, suspicion*
L'agent de police regarde le criminel avec méfiance.
The inspector is looking at the criminal with mistrust.

méfier, se   *to mistrust*
Je me méfie des gens qui ne me regardent pas quand ils me parlent.
I mistrust people who don't look at me when they're talking to me.

mégot m. *cigarette butt*
Quelle horreur! Elle a trouvé un mégot dans sa salade.
What a nightmare! She found a cigarette butt in her salad.

mégoter *to skimp on*
Ne mégote pas sur le vin, il y aura presque 200 invités!
Don't skimp on the wine; there'll be almost two hundred guests.

meilleur(e) *better*
Je trouve que cet hôtel est bien meilleur que l'autre.
I think this hotel is much better than the other one.

mêler, se *to meddle*
Il se mêle toujours de ma vie privée.
He's always meddling in my private life.

membre m. *member*
Il n'est plus membre de notre club.
He's no longer a member of our club.

même *even, same*
Tu as le même problème que moi; tu es fauché!
You have the same problem as me—you're broke!

mensonge m. *lie*
Le candidat ne fait que dire des mensonges.
The candidate is only telling lies.

mépris m. *contempt*
J'ai beaucoup de mépris pour lui et ses idées.
I have a lot of contempt for him and his ideas.

mer f. *sea*
Notre hôtel est près de la mer.
Our hotel is near the sea.

mercatique f. *marketing*
Je m'intéresse à la mercatique.
I'm interested in marketing.

merci *thanks*
On dit "merci" quand on reçoit un cadeau.
One says "thanks" when receiving a present.

mériter *to deserve*
C'est une employée qui ne mérite aucune augmentation de
salaire; elle est nulle!
She's an employee who doesn't deserve a raise at all; she's a loser!

message m.   *message*
On vient de recevoir un message urgent pour vous.
We just received an urgent message for you.

méthode f.   *method, way*
Le prof utilise une drôle de méthode pédagogique avec ses
    étudiants.
The professor is using an odd pedagogical method with his students.

mètre m.   *meter*
L'arrêt de bus est à 200 mètres d'ici.
The bus stop is 200 meters from here.

métro m.   *subway*
On a pris le métro pour aller à Montmartre.
We took the subway to go to Montmartre.

mets m. pl.   *dishes, delicacies*
On a assisté à un dîner où on a goûté des douzaines de mets
    internationaux.
We went to a dinner where we sampled dozens of international dishes.

mettre   *to put, to place, to wear*
Tu peux mettre ces fleurs dans un vase?
Can you put these flowers in a vase?
Tu mets quoi pour la fête?
What are you wearing to the party?

meubles f. pl.   *furniture*
J'espère remplacer toutes ces meubles vétustes.
I hope to replace all of this outdated furniture.

Midi, le m.   *the South of France*
Elle va visiter le Midi cet été.
She going to visit the South of France this summer.

miel m.   *honey*
J'achète toujours du miel local; c'est très efficace contre les
    allergies.
I always buy local honey; it's very effective against allergies.

mien(-enne) m. (f.)   *mine*
Ce livre est à toi? Oui, c'est le mien.
Is this book yours? Yes, it's mine.
C'est à qui, cette jupe? C'est la mienne.
Whose skirt is this? It's mine.

mieux   *better*
Il chante beaucoup mieux que moi; je n'ai pas l'oreille musicale.
He sings much better than I do; I don't have a musical ear.

mièvre   *mushy, cloying*
Je ne peux pas supporter son parfum mièvre!
I can't stand her cloying perfume.

mignon(-ne)   *cute*
Son copain est très mignon et il le sait.
His boyfriend is really cute, and he knows it.

mijoter   *to simmer*
Vous n'avez qu'à mijoter ce ragoût une heure et il sera prêt.
You only have to simmer this stew for an hour and it will be ready.

mille m.   *thousand*
Tu me dois mille dollars, tu sais.
You owe me a thousand dollars, you know.

minable   *pathetic, crummy*
Je trouve ton effort vraiment minable!
I find your effort to be really pathetic!

mince   *thin, slender*
Comme elle est très mince, je pense que cette robe serait trop
    grande pour elle.
*Because she's really slender, I think this dress would be too big
    for her.*

minorer   *to undervalue, to cut*
Le candidat déclare qu'il veut minorer les impôts, mais on verra
    bien ce qu'il fera une fois élu.
*The candidate says he wants to cut taxes, but we'll see what he does
    once he's elected.*

minorité f.   *minority*
Ceux qui n'aiment pas la glace au chocolat sont en minorité.
Those who don't like chocolate ice cream are in the minority.

minuit m.   *midnight*
Cendrillon a dû rentrer chez elle avant minuit.
Cinderella needed to be home before midnight.

miracle m.   *miracle*
Par je ne sais quel miracle, notre équipe a gagné le match.
By some miracle, our team won the game.

miraud(e)   *near-sighted*
Mon oncle est miraud; il ne voit rien sans lunettes.
My uncle is near-sighted; he can't see anything without glasses.

misère f.   *poverty, destitution*
Malheureusement, beaucoup de familles vivent dans la misère.
Unfortunately, a lot of families live in poverty.

moche   *ugly*
Ce canapé est trop moche, jetons-le!
This couch is too ugly—let's throw it out!

mode f.   *style, fashion*
Ces gants ne sont plus à la mode.
These gloves are no longer in style.

moi m.   *me, the self*
Donnez-moi une idée de ce que vous voulez.
Give me an idea of what you want.
Elle écrit une thèse sur de thème du moi dans l'art romantique.
She's writing a thesis on the theme of the self in Romantic art.

moindre, le/la   *the least*
Ça, c'est le moindre de tes problèmes!
That's the least of your problems!

moins, de   *less*
Elles ont beaucoup moins d'espace que nous.
They have a lot less space than we do.

mois m.   *month*
On viendra chez vous le mois prochain.
We'll come to your place next month.

moitié, à f.   *half*
J'étais à moitié endormi quand il a téléphoné.
I was half-asleep when he called.

moitié, la f.   *half of*
Il ne reste que la moitié du travail à faire.
Only half of the work remains to be done.

môme m. or f.   *(colloquial) kid, brat*
La fête aurait été bien plus agréable sans tous ces mômes.
The party would have been a lot better without all these kids.

moment m.   *moment, time, a while*
Ça va prendre un bon moment, tu sais.
It's going to take a while, you know.

mon, (ma, mes) m. (f., pl.)   *my*
Mon ami est très comique.
My friend is really funny.
Ma mère habite en Islande.
My mother lives in Iceland.
Je vais rendre visite à mes amis espagnols à Barcelone.
I'm going to visit my Spanish friends in Barcelona.

monde m.   *world*
Le monde est si vaste.
The world is so huge.

monnaie f.   *currency, change*
Est-ce que je peux faire de la monnaie, s'il vous plaît?
Can I get some change, please?

Monsieur m.   *mister, sir*
Monsieur, je peux vous aider?
Sir, may I help you?

montagne f.   *mountain*
Ils vont à la montagne pour faire du ski.
They're going to go skiing in the mountains.

monter   *to go up, to take something up*
Ok, je vais monter.
Ok, I'm going upstairs.
Tu peux monter la lessive?
Can you take the laundry up?

montre f.   *watch*
Comme cadeau, elle espère acheter une montre suisse à son oncle.
She hopes to buy her uncle a Swiss watch for a gift.

montrer   *to show*
Pouvez-vous nous montrer cette montre-ci?
Can you show us this watch?

morals f.   *morals*
Le dirigeant despotique était un homme sans morale.
The despotic leader was a man without morals.

moralité f.   *morality*
Elle parle constamment de la moralité.
She's always talking about morality.

morceau m.   *a piece of*
Tu veux un morceau de gâteau?
Do you want a piece of cake?

mordant(e)   *biting, stinging, caustic*
Il a vraiment un esprit mordant.
He really has a biting wit.

mordiller   *to nibble on, to chew*
Ne mordille pas ta manche!
Don't chew on your sleeve!

mordre   *to bite*
Attention au chien, il mord!
Watch out for the dog—it bites!

morne   *dreary, gloomy*
Je déteste le paysage morne de cette région.
I hate the dreary landscape of this region.

mort(e)   *dead*
Notre chatton est mort ce matin d'une maladie mystérieuse.
Our kitten died this morning from a mysterious illness.

mosquée f.   *mosque*
J'admire l'architecture de cette mosquée médiévale.
I admire the architecture of this medieval mosque.

mot m.   *word*
Je ne connais pas ce mot.
I don't know this word.

motif m.   *reason, motive, pattern*
Je pense qu'il a un motif caché.
I think he has a hidden motive.

moto f.   *motorcycle*
Il est venu à pied? Non, à moto.
Did he come on foot? No, he came by motorcycle.

mou(-olle)   *soft, listless, flabby*
Les guimauves qu'elle a apportées sont très molles.
The marshmallows she brought are very soft.

mouchoir m.   *handkerchief, tissue*
Donne-moi un mouchoir pour que je puisse me moucher.
Give me a tissue so I can blow my nose.

mouillé(e)   *wet, moist*
Tu ne peux pas porter ton maillot de bain au restaurant,
il est tout mouillé.
*You can't wear your bathing suit to the restaurant; it's completely
wet.*

mourir   *to die*
Le soldat a révélé au journaliste qu'il a peur de mourir sur le
champ de bataille.
*The soldier admitted to the journalist that he's afraid of dying on the
battlefield.*

moutard m.   *(colloquial) kid, brat*
Ce moutard me tape sur les nerfs. Ses parents arrivent quand?
This brat is getting on my nerves. When do his parents get here?

mouvementé(e)   *eventful, hectic*
Les trois dernières semaines du semestre sont toujours très
mouvementées.
The last three weeks of the semester are always very hectic.

mouvoir   *to put into motion*
Le mécanisme est mû par un simple ressort.
The mechanism is put into motion by a simple spring.

moyen m.   *means, way*
Par quel moyen espérez-vous le convaincre?
By what means do you hope to convince him?

moyen(-ne)   *medium*
Elle est de taille moyenne.
She's medium sized.

muer, se   *to transform oneself, to be transformed*
L'actrice se mue en paysanne du XIXième siècle pour son rôle.
*The actress is transforming herself into a nineteenth-century peasant
for her role.*

mur m.   *wall*
Les ouvriers recontruisent le mur qui a été détruit par l'orage.
The workers are rebuilding the wall that was destroyed by the storm.

mûr(e)   *ripe, mature*
Les raisins sont trop mûrs pour les manger.
The grapes are too ripe to eat.

musclé(e)   *muscular*
Elle est très musclée parce qu'elle fait des haltères trois fois par
   semaine.
She's very muscular because she lifts weights three times a week.

musée m.   *museum*
Notre ville vient d'ouvrir un musée municipal qui contient une
   grande collection.
Our city just opened a muncipal museum that houses a huge collection.

musique f.   *music*
Elle apprécie toutes sortes de musique.
She appreciates all types of music.

muter   *to transfer*
Notre entreprise va muter la plupart de ses employés en banlieue.
Our company is transferring most of its employees to the suburbs.

myope   *near-sighted, short-sighted*
Elle ne voit rien; elle est myope.
She can't see anything; she's near-sighted.

N

nager   *to swim*
Si vous aimez nager, allez à la piscine près d'ici, elle est très
   agréable.
If you like to swim, go to the pool near here; it's quite nice.

naguère   *not long ago, quite recently*
C'est une pratique qui était naguère très mal vue.
This is a practice that was up until recently looked down upon.

naïf(-ve)   *naïve*
Caroline est une fille naïve qui se fait duper par tout le monde.
Caroline is a naïve girl who is fooled by everyone.

narguer   *to taunt*
Il y a pas mal de rivaux qui me narguent.
There are quite a few rivals who taunt me.

navet m.   *turnip; dud or turkey (film, book)*
Le nouveau film de ce cinéaste est un vrai navet.
The new movie by this filmmaker is a real turkey.

navette f.   *shuttle*
Je prendrai la navette de l'aéroport à l'hôtel.
I will take the shuttle from the airport to the hotel.

naviguer   *to navigate*
Je peux très bien naviguer avec mon GPS.
I can navigate quite well with my GPS.

navré(e)   *sorry*
Je suis navré de te dire que je ne peux pas assister à ta fête.
I'm sorry to tell you that I can't come to your party.

né(e), être   *to be born*
Je suis né à Dakar en 1965.
I was born in Dakar in 1965.

ne...ni...ni   *neither...nor*
Je n'ai ni frère ni sœur.
I have neither a sister nor a brother.

néanmoins   *nevertheless, yet*
Elle le déteste, mais elle va néanmoins continuer à étudier le grec.
She hates it, but she is nevertheless going to continue studying Greek.

nécessaire   *necessary*
Il est nécessaire que tu fasses un plus grand effort.
It's necessary that you make a greater effort.

nécessairement   *necessarily, inevitably*
Cette idée n'est pas nécessairement bonne.
This idea isn't necessarily a good one.

neige f.   *snow*
J'aime bien la neige mais j'ai horreur du froid.
I like the snow but I hate the cold.

neiger   *to snow*
Selon les prévisions météo, il va neiger pendant deux jours de
    suite.
*According to the weather forecast, it's going to snow for two days in a
    row.*

nerfs m. pl.   *nerves*
Qu'est-ce qu'il me tape sur les nerfs!
Oh, how he grates on my nerves!

nerveux(-euse)   *nervous*
Elle devient très nerveuse avant de parler à ses profs.
She becomes quite nervous before speaking to her teachers.

net(-te)   *net; marked, clearcut*
Quel est le prix net de cette voiture?
What's the net price of this car?
On constate un changement net dans son comportement.
We see a marked change in his behaviour.

nettoyer   *to clean*
Vous devez nettoyer la salle de bain avant l'arrivée des invités.
You need to clean the bathroom before the guests arrive.

nez m.   *nose*
Elle est très jolie malgré son nez retroussé.
She's quite pretty despite her snub nose.

niais(e)   *stupid, idiotic*
On en a marre des commentaires niais de notre patron.
We are so sick of our boss's idiotic comments.

nier   *to deny*
Est-ce que tu es prête à nier l'existence des OVNI?
Are you ready to deny the existence of UFOs?

niveau m.   *level*
Ce cours est à un niveau débutant.
This course is at a beginner's level.

nocif(-ve)   *harmful, noxious*
Il y a beaucoup de produits chimiques qui sont très nocifs.
There are many chemicals that are quite harmful.

noël m.   *Christmas*
Joyeux Noël!
Merry Christmas!

noir(e)   *black*
Je vais mettre un pull noir avec un jean délavé.
I'm going to wear a black sweater with stone-washed jeans.

noisette f. *hazelnut, hazel*
Elle a fait une tarte aux noisettes.
She made a hazelnut tart.
Il a de très jolis yeux noisette.
He has beautiful hazel eyes.

noix f. pl. *nuts, walnuts*
Ma cousine est allergique à toutes sortes de noix.
My cousin is allergic to all kinds of nuts.

nom m. *name*
Quel est votre nom?
What is your name?

nombre m. *number*
Il y a un très grand nombre d'étudiants qui veut étudier en
France cette année.
*There is a great number of students who want to study in France this
year.*

nombreux(-euse) *numerous*
Il y a de nombreuses raisons pour lesquelles ce projet va réussir.
There are many reasons why this project will succeed.

nombriliste *egocentrist, self-centered*
Il est très intelligent mais un peu trop nombriliste.
He's very intelligent but a bit too self-centered.

non *no*
Tu peux me prêter de l'argent? Non, non et non!
Can you lend me some money? No, no, and no!

non plus *neither*
Je n'aime pas beaucoup le poulet. Moi non plus.
I don't like chicken. Neither do I.

normal(e) *normal*
Il n'est pas normal que tu ne manges qu'une fois par jour.
It's not normal that you only eat once a day.

normalement *normally*
Normalement on voit beaucoup de touristes ici, mais cette année
ils sont moins nombreux.
Normally we see a lot of tourists here but this year there are fewer.

note f.   *mark, grade*
Je viens d'avoir ma note et j'en suis content; j'ai eu 17 sur 20!
I just received my grade and I am very happy with it; I got 17 out of 20!

notre(nos) m. or f. (pl.)   *our*
Notre chien aboie constamment quand il est en laisse! Nos voi-
sins doivent nous détester!
Our dog constantly barks on the leash! Our neighbors must hate us!

nourriture f.   *food*
Mes enfants adorent la nourriture japonaise.
My kids love Japanese food.

nous   *we, us,*
Nous voudrions vous téléphoner. Vous pouvez nous donner
votre numéro de téléphone?
We would like to call you. Can you give us your phone number?

nouveau(-elle)   *new*
Je vous présente mon nouveau coloc, Jean-Pierre.
Let me introduce my new roommate, Jean-Pierre.
Avez-vous une nouvelle adresse?
Do you have a new address?

nouvelles f. pl.   *news*
As-tu appris les nouvelles? Paul et Virginie divorcent.
Have you heard the news? Paul and Virginia are getting divorced.

nuage m.   *cloud*
Il y a beaucoup de nuages dans le ciel, va-t-il faire un orage?
There are a lot of clouds in the sky; is it going to storm?

nuageux(-euse)   *cloudy*
Le ciel devient de plus en plus nuageux.
The sky is becoming cloudier and cloudier.

nuée f.   *swarm*
On marchait dans la forêt quand on a été soudainement attaqués
par une nuée d'abeilles.
*We were walking in the forest when all of a sudden we were attacked by
a swarm of bees.*

nuit f.   *night*
Je ne sors jamais la nuit.
I never go out at night.

nuitée f.   *overnight stay*
On a payé trois nuitées mais comme l'hôtel était désagréable, on
   est parti après deux jours.
*We paid for three overnight stays but since the hotel was unpleasant, we
   left after two days.*

nul(-le)   *hopeless, worthless, invalid*
Ce film est nul!
This movie is worthless!

numéro m.   *number*
Quel est ton numéro de portable?
What's your cellphone number?

nunuche   *(colloquial) silly, nutty, bird-brained*
Il ne faut pas écouter ce que Mathieu dit, il est vraiment
   nunuche.
Don't listen to what Matthew says, he's really silly.

O

obéir   *to obey*
Il faut obéir aux lois du pays, sinon on risque de se faire arrêter.
One must obey the laws of the land; if not one risks being arrested.

objet m.   *object*
Cet objet sert à quoi?
What is this object for?

obligé(e)   *obliged*
Est-ce qu'on est obligé de lui dire que nos parents n'assisteront
   pas à la fête?
*Are we obliged to tell them that our parents won't be coming to the
   party?*

obliger   *to obligate, to compel, to require*
Qu'est-ce qui t'oblige à faire cette remarque?
What is compelling you to make this remark?

obstiner, s'   *to stubbornly insist*
L'infirmier lui a dit de rester au lit, mais Madame Desroches
   s'obstine à faire la cuisine.
*The nurse told her to stay in bed, but Mrs. Desroches insists upon
   cooking.*

obtenir   *to obtain, to get*
Mon fils espère obtenir son permis de conduire cet été.
My son is hoping to get his driver's license this summer.

occasion f.   *event, opportunity*
Notre visite nous donne l'occasion de voir un ami qui habite ici
    depuis longtemps.
Our visit is giving us the opportunity to see a friend who has lived here
    for a long time.

Occident m.   *the West*
Ces réfugiés ont quitté leur pays pour venir en Occident.
These refugees left their country to come to the West.

occupé(e)   *busy*
Je suis très occupé en ce moment.
I'm very busy at the moment.

océan m.   *ocean*
Elle étudie l'effet du changement climatique sur les océans.
She is studying the effect of climate change on the oceans.

odeur f.   *odor, smell*
Il adore l'odeur de mon parfum.
He loves the smell of my perfume.

odieux (-ieuse)   *odious, heinous, obnoxious*
Je le déteste parce qu'il est odieux et cruel.
I hate him because he's obnoxious and cruel.

œil(yeux) m. (pl.)   *eye*
Mon oncle a un œil de verre et une jambe de bois.
My uncle has a glass eye and a wooden leg.

œuf m.   *egg*
Normalement le matin je prends un œuf à la coque.
In the morning I usually have a soft-boiled egg.

œuvre f.   *work of art, body of work*
J'ai lu toutes les œuvres de Zola; c'est mon écrivain préféré.
I've read Zola's body of work; he's my favorite writer.

oignon m.   *onion*
Mon fils refuse de manger des onions, ça m'embête!
My son refuses to eat onions; it bugs me!

oiseau(æ) m. (pl.)   *bird*
Il n'y a rien de plus agréable que le chant des oiseaux que l'on
entend chez nous le matin.
*There's nothing more beautiful than the morning birdsong that we hear
at our house.*

ombre f.   *shadow, shade*
Tu dois mettre ton bébé à l'ombre; le soleil est très fort
aujourd'hui.
You should put your baby in the shade; the sun is really strong today.

omelette f.   *omelet*
Elle nous a servi une délicieuse omelette aux champignons.
She served us a delicious mushroom omelet.

ondulé(e)   *wavy*
Elle a des cheveux ondulés.
She has wavy hair.

or m.   *gold*
Cette bague en or blanc est magnifique, où tu l'as trouvée?
This white-gold ring is fabulous; where did you find it?

ordinateur m.   *computer*
Elle a acheté un nouvel ordinateur en ligne.
She bought a new computer online.

ordonnance f.   *prescription*
Est-ce que j'ai besoin d'une ordonnance pour avoir ces gouttes?
Do I need a prescription to get these drops?

ordre m.   *order*
Elle a mis tout en ordre avant son départ.
She put everything in order before her departure.

oreille f.   *ear*
Elle a trois piercings à l'oreille.
She has three piercings in her ear.

oreiller m.   *pillow*
Je préfère dormir sans oreiller.
I prefer to sleep without a pillow.

orgueil m.   *arrogance, pride*
Il vous a parlé de cette manière? Quel orgueil!
He spoke to you like that? What arrogance!

os m. *bone*
Notre chien aime bien ronger les os.
Our dog loves to gnaw on bones.

oser *to dare*
Je n'ose pas lui dire la vérité.
I don't dare tell him the truth.

ou *or*
Qu'est-ce que tu aimes mieux—les chats ou les chiens?
Which do you prefer, cats or dogs?

où *where*
Tu vas où?
Where are you going?

ouais *yeah (informal)*
Tu me donnes une cigarette? Ouais, ok.
Can you give me a cigarette? Yeah, ok.

oublier *to forget*
Elle a tendance à oublier ses clés chez moi.
She has a tendency to forget her keys at my place.

oui *yes*
Vous parlez français? Oui, bien sûr.
Do you speak French? Yes, of course.

outil m. *tool*
Il aimerait bien réparer sa voiture mais il a besoin d'autres
    outils.
He'd like to fix his car, but he needs other tools.

ouvert(e) *open*
Le musée sera ouvert de midi à minuit.
The museum will be open from noon to midnight.

ouvrage m. *work, book*
Un nouvel ouvrage de mon poète préféré vient de paraître il y a
    quelques semaines.
A new book by my favorite poet was just published a few weeks ago.

ouvrier(-ière) m (f.) *worker*
Mon père est ouvrier et membre de ce syndicat.
My dad is a worker and a member of this union.

ouvrir   *to open*
Elle rêve d'ouvrir un petit restaurant dans cet immeuble.
She dreams of opening a small restaurant in this building.

P

PACS m.   *"pacte civil de solidarité" (civil union in France)*
Les partenaires liés par PACS bénéficient de nombreux droits.
Partners who are joined in a PACS are entitled to numerous rights.

pagaille f.   *mess, shambles, chaos*
Je ne veux pas que tu viennes chez moi, c'est la pagaille.
I don't want you to come over; it's a mess.

pain m.   *bread*
Il est essentiel de servir ce plateau de fromage avec beaucoup
de pain.
It's vital to serve this cheese plate with a lot of bread.

paire f.   *pair*
Elle a tricoté une jolie paire de chaussettes.
She knitted a beautiful pair of socks.

paix f.   *peace*
Nous somme tous pour la paix entre ces deux pays.
We are all for peace between these two countries.

palais m.   *palace*
Les touristes ont envie de voir le palais royal.
The tourists are eager to see the royal palace.

pâle   *pale*
J'ai su qu'elle était malade quand je l'ai vue devenir toute pale.
I figured out that she was sick when I saw her become totally pale.

pantalon m.   *pants*
Il a acheté un pantalon bleu.
He bought a pair of blue pants.

pantouflard(e)   *lazybones, homebody*
Comme il est pantouflard il aime bien rester à la maison.
As he's a homebody, he likes to stay at home.

papier m.   *paper*
Donne-moi du papier pour mon imprimante.
Give me some paper for my printer.

paquet m.   *pack, packet*
Ce paquet de cigarettes m'a coûté presque $10!
This pack of cigarettes cost me nearly ten dollars!

par   *by*
Elle est passée par le marché en rentrant.
She stopped by the market on her way home.

parages m. pl.   *the vicinity*
Où est Claire? Elle est dans les parages.
Where's Claire? She's somewhere in the vicinity.

paragraphe m.   *paragraph*
Ce paragraphe-ci est trop long, il faut le raccourcir.
This paragraph is too long; it must be shortened.

paraît que, il   *It appears that*
Il paraît que les enfants aiment bien ce film.
It appears that kids love this film.

paraître   *to appear, to show*
Il ne laisse rien paraître de ses sentiments.
He doesn't let his feelings show at all.

parapluie m.   *umbrella*
Prends ton parapluie parce qu'il va certainement pleuvoir
aujourd'hui.
Take your umbrella because it's certainly going to rain today.

parc m.   *park*
Ce printemps on espère visiter quelques parcs nationaux et faire
du camping.
This spring we hope to visit a few parks and do some camping.

parce que   *because*
Je l'aime bien parce qu'elle est généreuse.
I like her because she's generous.

pardonner   *to excuse, to forgive*
Il faut le pardonner, il ne sait pas ce qu'il dit.
You must excuse him; he doesn't know what he's saying.

parent(e)   *relative, relation, parent*
Je suis parent avec elle.
I am her relative.

paresseux(-euse)   *lazy*
Elles sont intelligentes mais aussi paresseuses.
They are intelligent, but also lazy.

parfois   *sometimes*
Parfois je me balade dans mon jardin quand je m'ennuie.
Sometimes I go for a stroll in my garden when I am bored.

parler   *to speak, talk*
Je dois te parler.
I need to talk to you.

parmi   *among*
Il semble toujours y avoir de la mauvaise herbe parmi les fleurs.
There always seem to be weeds among the flowers.

parole f.   *speech, word, promise*
J'aime bien cette chanson mais j'ai oublié les paroles.
I like this song but I've forgotten the words.

parti m.   *political party*
Elle s'intéresse aux idées de ce parti.
She's very interested in the ideas of this party.

partie f.   *part*
La meilleure partie de ce film est la fin—tout explose!
The best part of this movie is the end—everything explodes!

partout   *all over, everywhere*
Elles ont voyagé ensemble partout en Europe.
They traveled together all over Europe.

parvenir   *to arrive at, to come about*
Pouvez-vous nous expliquer comment vous êtes parvenu à ces calculs?
Can you explain to us how you arrived at these calculations?

pas   *negation*
Elle (n')a pas faim.
She isn't hungry.
Note: *The (ne) of the negation is rarely pronounced in spoken French.*

pas m.   *step*
Tu fais un pas en arrière.
You are taking a step back.

passer   *to spend, to pass, to stop by*
On va passer quelques semaines en Tunisie.
We're going to spend a few weeks in Tunisia.

pastille f.   *lozenge*
J'aime ces pastilles à l'anis.
I love these anise lozenges.

(et) patati et patata   *and so on and so forth, blah blah blah*
Il a dit qu'il était navré mais qu'il devait travailler et patati et
   patata.
He said he was sorry but that he had to work, blah blah blah.

pâtes f. pl.   *pasta*
Elle leur a servi des pâtes à l'huile d'olive.
She served them pasta with olive oil.

patron(-ne) m. (f.)   *boss*
Notre patron ne travaille que trois heures par jour.
Our boss works only three hours a day.

paumé(e)   *lost, at loose ends*
Le pauvre gamin est un peu paumé après la mort de son chiot.
The poor kid is at loose ends after the death of his puppy.

pauvre   *poor*
La famille de mon mari est très pauvre donc ils vont venir habiter
   chez nous.
My husband's family is quite poor so they're going to come live with us.

payer   *to pay à*
On a déjà trop payé pour cet hôtel exécrable!
We've already paid too much for this horrendous hotel!

payer, se faire   *to get paid for*
Il se fait payer combien pour son travail?
How much does he get paid for his work?

pays m.   *land, country*
Vous êtes de quel pays?
What country are you from?

paysage m.   *landscape*
Les artistes aiment bien venir ici pour dessiner ce paysage serein.
Artists like to come here to draw this tranquil landscape.

PDG   *CEO*
Je viens de faire la connaissance de notre nouveau PDG; il a l'air
   très gentil.
I just met our new CEO; he seems very nice.

peau f.   *skin*
La peau du visage de mon oncle est ridée.
The skin on my uncle's face is wrinkled.

peaufiner   *to polish, to put the finishing touches on*
Elle est en train de peaufiner son recueil de poésie.
*She's in the midst of putting the finishing touches on her collection
   of poetry.*

péché m.   *sin*
Tuer est un péché mortel.
To kill is a mortal sin.

pêche f.   *peach*
On a servi du thé froid à la pêche et c'était délicieux.
We served peach iced tea, and it was delicious.

pédaler   *to pedal*
Tu dois pédaler plus vite que ça!
You need to pedal faster than that!

peindre   *to paint*
Elle a suffisament d'argent pour peindre sa maison, mais elle ne
   veut pas le faire.
She has enough money to paint her house, but she doesn't want to do it.

peine f.   *sorrow, grief*
Il a beaucoup de peine en ce moment.
He has a lot of sorrow at the moment.

peine, à   *hardly*
On était à la fête depuis à peine dix minutes quand on a reçu un
   coup de fil de notre babysitter nous demandant de renter.
*We had hardly been at the party for ten minutes when we got a call
   from our babysitter asking us to come home.*

peinture f.   *painting*
J'aime bien la peinture italienne.
I like Italian painting.

pelouse f.   *lawn, grass*
Quand je voyage je demande à mon voisin de s'occuper de ma
   pelouse.
When I travel I ask my neighbor to take care of my lawn.

pendant   *during*
Elle a pleuré pendant toute la pièce de théâtre.
She cried during the entire play.

penser   *to think*
Qu'est-ce que tu penses de la situation actuelle?
What do you think about the current situation?

pension f.   *pension*
Il reçoit une pension de l'état.
He receives a pension from the state.

pente f.   *slope, path*
Sa maison a un toit en pente.
His house has a sloping roof.
Pense à mettre le frein à main en pente.
Think about putting the hand brake on on a slope.

pépère   *(colloquial) old-fashioned seeming, "grandmotherly"*
Quel appart pépère!
What an old-fashioned apartment!

percuter   *to hit something, to crash into something*
Elle a percuté un passant avec son vélo.
She hit a passer-by with her bike.

perdre   *to lose*
Notre équipe va certainement perdre ce soir.
Our team is certainly going to lose tonight.

périmé(e)   *out-of-date, expired*
Malheureusement, mon passeport est périmé.
Unfortunately, my passport has expired.

permettre   *to permit, to enable*
Ce nouveau logiciel va vous permettre de vite calculer vos impôts.
This new software will enable you to quickly calculate your taxes.

permission f.   *permission*
Avec votre permission, j'aimerais voir les dossiers des candidates.
With your permission, I'd like to see the candidates' files.

personne   *no one, nobody*
Personne ne demande l'impossible.
No one asks the impossible.

peser   *to weigh*
Elle pèse plus que vous.
She weighs more than you.

pétillant(e)   *sparkling*
Ma mère aime l'eau pétillante.
My mother likes sparkling water.

petit(e)   *small, little*
On a un petit problème.
We have a small problem.

peu   *few*
Monsieur Ducros a très peu d'amis.
Mister Ducros has very few friends.

peu, un   *a few, a bit*
Tu as soif? Oui, un peu.
Are you thirsty? Yes, a bit.

peur, avoir   *to be afraid*
L'enfant a peur des serpents.
The child is afraid of snakes.

peut-être   *maybe, perhaps*
Il y a peut-être près de 3 000 SDF dans cette ville.
The are perhaps close to 3,000 homeless people in this city.

phare m.   *headlight, beacon; primary, leading*
C'est un philosophe phare de sa génération.
He's a leading philosopher of his generation.

photo f.   *photo*
Quelle jolie photo!
What a pretty picture!

phrase f.   *sentence*
Le maître a écrit la phrase au tableau.
The teacher wrote the sentence on the board.

piauler   *to whimper, to simper*
Je ne supporte pas d'entendre piauler les enfants gâtés.
I can't stand hearing spoiled children whimpering.

pièce f.   *room*
Combien de pièces y-a-t-il dans cet appartement?
How many rooms are there in this apartment?

pied m.   *foot*
J'ai mal au pied.
My foot hurts.

piège m.   *trap*
Le criminel s'est laissé prendre au piège.
The criminal walked right into the trap.

pierre f.   *rock*
Que celui qui n'a jamais péché lui jette la première pierre.
Let he who is without blame cast the first stone.

piéton m.   *pedestrian*
Les piétons ne peuvent pas traverser la rue parce qu'il y a trop de circulation.
The pedestrians can't cross the street because there is too much traffic.

pif, au m.   *by guesswork, by feel*
On l'a fait au pif.
We did it by guesswork.

piger   *(colloquial) to get it, to understand*
Tout d'un coup, elle a tout pigé.
Suddenly she understood everything.

pile   *just, exactly, on the dot*
Je suis arrivé à neuf heures pile.
I arrived at nine on the dot.

piloter   *to drive, to pilot*
Il a piloté sa voiture à une vitesse de plus de 125 km/heure.
He drove his car at a speed of over 125 km an hour.

pilule f.   *pill, the Pill*
Elle prend la pilule depuis deux ans.
She's been taking the Pill for two years.

pimbêche, être une f.   *to be stuck up*
Madame Duval est une vraie pimbêche; elle refuse de nous parler.
Madame Duval is really stuck up; she refuses to talk to us.

piment m.   *red pepper, spice*
Parfois il faut faire certaines choses pour mettre du piment dans
   sa vie.
Sometimes you need to do certain things to put some spice in your life.

pimpant(e)   *spruced up, sporty, attractive*
Avec cette nouvelle voiture pimpante, tu vas certainement faire
   impression.
*With this sporty new car, you are certainly going to make an
   impression.*

pinailleur(-euse)   *nit-picking, fussy, persnickety*
Elle est si pinailleuse qu'elle va sans doûte rejeter toutes nos
   suggestions.
She's so fussy that she will no doubt reject all our suggestions.

pinard m.   *(colloquial) wine*
Du pinard, du pain et du fromage—il y'a pas mieux que ça!
Wine, bread, and cheese—it doesn't get better than that!

piquer   *to sting, to bite; to steal*
Les moustiques ici, ça pique!
The mosquitos here bite!
Qui a piqué mon fric?
Who stole my money?

piqûre f.   *injection, sting*
Notre fils aîné a très peur des piqûres; il déteste aller chez le
   médecin.
Our eldest son is really afraid of shots—he hates going to the doctor's.

pire   *worse*
Ils chantent pire que vous!
They sing worse than you!

piscine f.   *swimming pool*
On a fait construire une piscine chez mes parents.
We had a swimming pool built at my parents' house.

pittoresque   *picturesque*
Ce petit village est très pittoresque.
This little village is quite picturesque.

place f.   *place, seat, square*
Cette place est résérvée.
This seat is reserved.

plafond m.   *ceiling*
Le plafond de verre n'est pas un mythe, c'est vrai!
The glass ceiling isn't a myth, it's true!

plage f.   *beach*
Les enfants pourraient passer des semaines entières à la plage si leurs mères le permettaient.
Children would spent entire weeks at the beach if their mothers let them.

plaindre, se   *to complain*
On dit que les Français aiment se plaindre.
It is said that the French like to complain.

plainte f.   *complainte*
Si tu n'aimes pas le traitement que tu as reçu, tu dois porter plainte à la direction!
If you aren't pleased with the treatment you received, you should make a complaint to the management!

plaire   *to please*
Madame Roudier est très sévère; les élèves essaient de lui plaire mais elle n'est jamais satisfaite.
Mrs. Roudier is very strict; the students try to please her, but she's never satisfied.

plaisanterie f.   *joke*
Ne te fâche pas—c'était une plaisanterie!
Don't get mad—it was a joke!

plaisir m.   *pleasure*
Quel plaisir de vous voir!
What a pleasure to see you!

plancher m.   *floor*
Je ne sais pas comment nettoyer ce plancher en céramique.
I don't know how to clean this tile floor.

planer   *to glide; to hang over; to be high (intoxicated), to have one's head in the clouds*
Un sentiment de joie plane dans le pays depuis que le président a signé un pacte de paix.
A feeling of joy glides over the country since the president signed the peace treaty.
Il ne voit pas la réalité telle qu'elle est; il plane.
He doesn't see reality as it is; he has his head in the clouds.

planter   *to plant*
J'ai l'intention de planter des fleurs à côté de notre pavillon.
I'm planning on planting flowers next to our house.

planter, se   *(colloquial) to crash, to get it wrong*
Même avec l'aide de son prof, il s'est toujours planté en physique.
Even with the help of his teacher, he still did terribly in physics.

plat m.   *dish*
Ce restaurant sert de très bons plats végétariens.
This restaurant serves very good vegetarian dishes.

plat(e)   *flat*
Je trouve ce paysage plat un peu déprimant.
I find this flat landscape a bit depressing.

plein(e)   *full*
Le plein, s'il vous plaît!
Fill 'er up, please!

pleurer   *to cry*
L'enfant ne cesse jamais de pleurer, j'en peux plus!
The kid never stops crying—I can't take it anymore!

pleuvoir   *to rain*
Selon les prévisions météo, il va pleuvoir toute la journée.
According to the weather forecast, it's going to rain all day.

plier   *to fold*
Afin de mettre cette lettre dans l'envelope, il faut la plier.
In order to put this letter in the envelope, you need to fold it.

pluie f.   *rain*
Cette pluie m'embête.
This rain is getting to me.

plupart (de)   *most, majority*
La plupart des Parisiens n'ont pas de voiture.
The majority of Parisians don't have a car.

plus   *more*
Il y a plus de choix dans ce magasin que dans l'autre.
There are more choices in this store than in the other one.

plusieurs   *several*
Il y a plusieurs films qui m'intéressent en ce moment.
There are several films that interest me at the moment.

plutôt   *rather, somewhat*
Les cheveux de ma fille sont plutôt ondulés.
My daughter's hair is rather wavy.

poche f.   *pocket*
Mets tes clés dans ta poche.
Put your keys in your pocket.

poème m.   *poem*
J'ai envie d'écrire un poème pour mon ami.
I feel like writing a poem for my friend.

poids m.   *weight*
Il a perdu du poids récemment.
He lost weight recently.

poignarder   *to stab*
Le candidat a perdu toute sa crédibilité après avoir poignardé le
     journaliste.
The candidate lost all credibility after he stabbed the journalist.

point m.   *point*
Choisissons un point de rencontre.
Let's choose a meeting point.

pointer, se   *(colloquial) to turn up*
Il s'est pointé vers midi.
He turned up around noon.

poitrine f.   *chest*
Quel est ton tour de poitrine?
What is your chest size?

poli(e)   *polite*
C'est un homme très poli.
He's a very polite man.

police f.   *police*
Certains résidents de cette ville ont peur de la police.
Certain residents of this city are afraid of the police.

police f.   *font, typeface*
Notre enterprise nous encourage à utiliser cette police pour notre
     correspondance officielle.
*Our company is encouraging us to use this typeface for our official
     correspondence.*

polluer *to pollute*
Cette entreprise doit payer une amende car elle a pollué ce lac pendant dix ans.
This company has to pay a fine because it polluted this lake for ten years.

pollution f. *pollution*
Il y a de nombreuse villes dans ce pays où la pollution empêche les résidents de sortir.
There are numerous cities in this country in which pollution prevents residents from going outside.

pont m. *bridge*
Ce pont relie les deux parties du village.
This bridge connects the two parts of the village.

port m. *port*
Marseille est le port le plus actif de France.
Marseille is the most active port in France.

portable m. *cellphone, laptop*
Donne-moi ton portable pour que je puisse donner un coup de fil à Vincent.
Give me your cellphone so I can call Vincent.
J'emporte mon portable en vacances, comme ça je peux écrire mon roman.
I'm bringing my laptop on vacation so I can write my novel.

porte f. *door*
Entrons par la porte de devant.
Let's go in by the front door.

portefeuille m. *wallet*
Elle a offert un portefeuille en cuir à son père pour son anniversaire.
She gave her father a leather wallet for his birthday.

porter *to wear, to carry*
Il va porter un nouveau costume pour son entretien demain.
He's going to wear a new suit for his interview tomorrow.
Les passagers portent leurs bagages à bord.
The passengers are carrying their bags on board.

poser *to ask*
Je peux te poser une question?
Can I ask you a question?

poste m.   *position, job*
Il a trouvé un poste au Québec avec une enterprise internationale.
He found a job in Québec with an international company.

poste f.   *post office*
On peut acheter des timbres à la poste.
We can buy stamps at the post office.

pot, avoir du   *(colloquial) to be lucky*
Alors celui-là a vraiment du pot.
Boy, that guy is really lucky.

potasser   *(colloquial) to cram, to bone up*
Comme on a un examen de chimie demain, on doit vraiment
    potasser ce soir.
*Since we have a chemistry exam tomorrow, we have to really cram
    tonight.*

pote(-esse) m. (pl.)   *(colloquial) friend, pal*
Touche pas à mon pote!
*Keep your hands off my friend! (slogan of the social solidarity
    organization SOS Racisme)*

poupée f.   *doll*
Donne sa poupée à la gamine pour qu'elle arrête de pleurer.
Give the child her doll so she will stop crying.

pour   *for*
Tiens, le facteur a apporté une lettre pour toi.
Here you go, the letter carrier brought you a letter.

pourboire m.   *tip*
Les serveurs se plaignent des clients radins qui laissent des
    mauvais pourboires.
*The waiters are complaining about cheap customers who leave
    bad tips.*

pourquoi   *why*
Pourquoi es-tu si triste? Qu'est-ce qu'il y a?
Why are you so sad? What's wrong?

pourtant   *yet, even, though*
Je n'ai pas beaucoup de temps libre en ce moment pourtant j'ai
    quand même envie d'aller à la soirée.
*I don't have a lot of free time right now, yet I still feel like going to the
    party.*

pousser   *to push, to grow*
Pousse la porte pour l'ouvrir.
Push the door to open it.
Je me laisse pousser les cheveux.
I'm letting my hair grow.

pouvoir   *to be able to*
Pouvez-vous me téléphoner?
Are you able to call me?

préalable   *previous, preceding, preliminary*
Notre décision préalable vient d'être annulée.
Our previous decision was just nullified.

préconiser   *to strongly recommend, to advise*
Le directeur de l'établissement préconise l'exclusion immédiate
   de cet étudiant difficile.
*The school director strongly recommends the immediate expulsion of
   this difficult student.*

premièr(e)   *first*
C'est ma première visite ici.
It's my first visit here.

prendre   *to take, to have*
Ils vont prendre un vol de Montréal à Ottawa.
They're taking a flight from Montreal to Ottawa.
Elle prend son café en écoutant la radio.
She has her coffee while listening to the radio.

préparer   *to prepare*
Nous avons décidé de préparer un couscous pour nos invités.
We decided to prepare couscous for our guests.

près de   *near*
On cherche une maison près du parc.
We're looking for a house near the park.

presque   *almost*
Mes ancêtres habitent dans cette région depuis presque
   cent ans.
My ancestors have lived in this region for almost a hundred years.

pressé(e)   *in a hurry*
Le directeur ne peut pas nous parler parce qu'il est pressé.
The director can't talk to us because he's in a hurry.

pressentir   *to have a premonition, to sense*
On a tous pressenti l'arrivée de notre patron donc on a vite repris notre travail.
We all sensed the arrival of our boss, so we quickly got back to work.

prêter   *to lend*
Je refuse de vous prêter de l'argent.
I refuse to lend you money.

prévisible   *predictable, foreseeable*
Cette situation était pourtant prévisible.
However, this situation was foreseeable.

prévu(e)   *predicted, planned for*
Tout s'est passé comme prévu.
Everything happened as planned.

prime f.   *bonus, free gift*
Je vais te montrer le cadeau de la banque que j'ai reçu en prime.
I'm going to show you the free gift I received from the bank.

prison f.   *prison*
Elle risque d'être condamnée à deux ans de prisons.
She may be sentenced to two years in prison.

prix m.   *price*
Quel est le prix de ces billets?
What is the price of these tickets?

problème m.   *problem*
Il a trop de problèmes en ce moment.
He has too many problems at the moment.

prochain(e)   *next*
On se verra l'année prochaine.
We'll see each other next year.

prochainement   *soon, shortly*
Le nouveau numéro de notre revue de poésie sera disponible prochainement chez les libraries.
The new issue of our poetry magazine will be available soon in bookstores.

prof m.   *teacher, professor*
On a été très surpris de découvrir que notre prof de philo déteste lire!
We were very surprised to find out that our philosophy professor hates to read!

profit m.   *benefit, profit, advantage*
J'ai vendu ma maison avec profit.
I sold my house at a profit.

profiter de   *to take advantage of*
Il faut profiter du beau temps!
We have to take advantage of the beautiful weather!

projet m.   *project*
Nous attendons le financement pour notre projet.
We are waiting for the financing for our project.

promenade f.   *walk*
Faisons une promenade!
Let's take a walk!

promener   *to walk*
Il nous paie pour promener ses chiens.
He's paying us to walk his dogs.

promener, se   *to go on a walk*
Ils veulent se promener pour prendre l'air.
They want to go on a walk to get some fresh air.

promesse f.   *promise*
Il tient ses promesses.
He keeps his promises.

propre   *clean*
La chambre de mon fils est toujours très propre.
My son's room is always very clean.

propriétaire m. or f.   *owner*
Nous voulons contacter le propriétaire de ce terrain pour
   l'interviewer.
We want to contact the owner of this land to interview him.

propriété f.   *property*
La propriété privée est un droit assuré par notre constitution.
Private property is a right insured by our constitution.

proprio   *(colloquial) landlord, landlady*
Elle se dispute avec son proprio parce qu'il lui doit de l'argent
   pour les reparations qu'elle a faites.
*She's fighting with her landlord because he owes her money for the
   repairs she made.*

protéger   *to protect*
On dit que cette loi va protéger les animaux en voie de
     disparition.
It is said that this law is going to protect endangered animals.

provisoire   *temporary, provisional*
Je vous donne un mot de passe provisoire.
I am giving you a temporary password.

prudent(e)   *careful, prudent*
Il faut être prudent, ne prenez pas de risques!
You should be careful; don't take any risks!

publicité f.   *advertisement*
Je déteste cette chaîne, il y a toujours trop de publicités.
I hate this channel—there are always too many advertisements.

pudeur f.   *sense of modesty, decency*
Même si cette actrice est une très grande vedette, elle est connue
     pour sa pudeur.
Even if this actress is a big star, she is known for her sense of modesty.

puis   *then*
D'abord je suis allé au pressing et puis chez le fleuriste.
First I went to the dry cleaner's, and then to the flower shop.

Q

quai m.   *quay, pier, platform*
Les voyageurs attendent le train sur le quai.
The travelers are waiting for their train on the platform.

quand   *when*
Quand devez-vous partir?
When do you have to leave?

quant à   *as for, as far as … is concerned*
Quant à lui, je pense qu'il a eu tort d'avoir réagi d'une telle
     manière.
*As far as he is concerned, I think that he was wrong to have reacted in
     such a manner.*

quartier m.   *neighborhood*
Ce quartier est si délabré que je ne veux plus y vivre.
This neighborhood is so dilapidated that I don't want to live here any more.

quasiment   *(colloquial) practically*
Après cette défaite, notre équipe est quasiment éliminée du tournoi.
After this defeat, our team is practially eliminated from the tournament.

que   *what, that*
Le film que nous avons vu était ridicule.
The film that we saw was ridiculous.
Que voulez-vous dire?
What do you mean?

quelque chose   *something*
Il a quelque chose pour toi.
He has something for you.

quelque part   *somewhere*
Mon portable doit être ici quelque part.
My cellphone should be here somewhere.

quelques-uns (-unes) m. pl. (f. pl)   *some, a few*
J'en ai vu quelques-uns.
I saw a few of them.

quelqu'un   *someone*
Quelqu'un t'appelle.
Someone is calling you.

question f.   *question*
Elle essaie de répondre à votre question.
She's trying to answer your question.

questionner   *to question*
L'inspecteur de police veut questionner le suspect.
The inspector wants to question the suspect.

queue f.   *line, file*
Il faut faire la queue au guichet.
You have to wait in line at the ticket office.

qui   *who, whom*
Qui voulez-vous voir?
Whom do you wish to see?
Notre enterprise cherche quelqu'un qui puisse faire la comptabilité.
Our business is searching for someone who can do accounting.

quitter   *to leave*
On aimerait bien quitter cette ville, mais comment?
We'd love to leave this city, but how?

quoi   *what*
Tu veux que je fasse quoi?
You want me to do what?

R

rabais m.   *discount*
Il achète tout à rabais.
He buys everything at a discount.

rabioter   *to scrounge, to swindle, to mooch off of*
Attention! Elle rabiote à toutes les occasions.
Watch out! She mooches all the time

raccourci m.   *short cut*
Jean aime bien prendre des raccourcis, on se perd toujours.
Jean loves to take short cuts; we always get lost.

raconter   *to tell, to recount*
Racontez-nous l'histoire de votre voyage à Tanger.
Tell us the story of your trip to Tangiers.

radin(e)   *(colloquial) stingy, cheap*
Pierre est tellement radin qu'il ne laisse jamais de pourboire.
Pierre is so stingy that he never leaves a tip.

raffiné(e)   *refined, sophisticated*
C'est une femme raffinée qui a très bon goût.
She's a sophisticated woman who has very good taste.

raffoler...de   *to be crazy about*
Je raffole du chocolat!
I'm crazy about chocolate!

ragots m. pl.   *(colloquial) malicious gossip*
J'en ai vraiment marre des ragots, moi!
I'm really sick of malicious gossip!

ragoûtant(e)   *appetizing, savory*
C'était un repas peu ragoûtant.
It was an unappetizing meal.

raison f.   *reason*
Voici la raison pour laquelle je ne te parle plus: tu es trop égoïste!
Here's the reason why I don't talk to you any more—you're so selfish!

raison, avoir   *to be right*
Vous avez complètement raison.
You are totally right.

raisonner   *to reason*
Notre prof de philo nous parle de l'importance de raisonner de
     façon logique.
*Our philosophy teacher is discussing with us the importance of logical
     reasoning.*

ralentir   *to slow down*
Ralentissons un peu; la chaussée est glissante à cause de
     la pluie.
Let's slow down a bit; the road is slippery because of the rain.

râler   *(colloquial) to moan, to grumble*
Les élèves ont commencé à râler quand le maître leur a annoncé
     l'épreuve du lendemain.
*The students started to moan when the teacher told them about the next
     day's test.*

ramer   *(colloquial) to work hard, to slog*
On rame, on a l'impression de ne pas avancer.
We're working hard, but we feel like we're not moving forward.

rancune f.   *resentment, grudge*
Pourquoi vivre avec tant de rancune dans ton cœur?
Why live with so much resentment in your heart?

randonnée f.   *hike, hiking*
Faisons une randonnée après le déjeuner.
Let's take a hike after lunch.

ranger   *to put away, to put into order*
Rangez vos jouets ou vous resterez à l'intérieur pour le reste de
     l'après-midi!
Put your toys away, or you'll stay inside for the rest of the afternoon!

rapide   *fast*
Voilà le train le plus rapide du monde.
Here's the fastest train in the world.

rapidement   *quickly*
Elle parle si rapidement que ses élèves ne peuvent pas la suivre.
She talks so quickly that her students can't follow her.

rappeler   *to remind*
Pouvez-vous me rappeller votre nom?
Can you remind me of your name?

raser, se   *to shave oneself*
Mon frère ne se rase jamais, il se dit contre!
My brother never shaves; he says he's against it!

rater   *to fail*
Elle est sur le point de rater tous ses examens.
She's about to fail all her exams.

raturer   *to cross out, to alter, to erase*
Qui a raturé mon nom de la liste?
Who crossed my name off the list?

ravi(e)   *thrilled, delighted*
Elle est ravie de voir le match de tennis de son fils.
She is delighted to see her son's tennis match.

rébarbatif (-ive)   *daunting, forbidding*
J'ai peur que ce travail devienne de plus en plus rébarbatif.
I fear that this work is becoming more and more daunting.

rebours, à   *backwards*
Le gamin compte à rebours: 5, 4, 3,...
The child is counting backwards: 5, 4, 3,...

recette f.   *recipe*
Quand j'étais petite, ma mère faisait des petits gâteaux délicieux,
    mais j'ai perdu la recette.
When I was little, my mother made delcious cookies, but I've lost the recipe.

recevoir   *to receive, to get*
Elle espère recevoir beaucoup de cadeaux pour son anniversaire.
She hopes to get a lot of gifts for her birthday.

réclamer   *to call for, to claim, to demand*
Après tant de promesses non-tenues par l'entreprise qui a
    fabriqué un produit inférieur, de nombreux consommateurs
    réclament leur dû.
*After so many broken promises by the company that made the faulty
    product, many consumers are demanding their due.*

reconnaître   *to recognize*
Ta barbe est si longue que l'on ne te reconnaît plus!
Your beard is so long that we no longer recognize you!

reçu m.   *receipt*
J'ai perdu un reçu dont j'ai besoin pour mon travail.
I lost a receipt that I need for my work.

recul m.   *detachment, standing back*
Je comprends ta colère, mais si tu prends du recul, tu verras que
   la décision est la bonne.
*I understand your anger, but if you step back, you'll see that the deci-
   sion is the right one.*

rédaction f.   *writing, essay, composition*
La rédaction est à rendre le 23 mai.
The composition is due May 23rd.

rédiger   *to write, to draft*
L'avocat est en train de rédiger notre contrat.
The lawyer is in the midst of drawing up our contract.

redoubler   *to repeat a year; to intensify*
C'est le cancre de la classe, il doit redoubler l'année.
He's the dunce of the class—he has to repeat the year.
Redoublons nos efforts pour que le projet soit résussi.
Let's intensify our efforts so the project will be a success.

redouté(e)   *feared*
C'est le prof le plus redouté de notre lycée.
He's the most feared teacher in our high school.

régaler   *to treat, to regale*
Régale-nous avec tes histoires!
Regale us with your stories!

regarder   *to watch*
Tu veux regarder un film avec moi?
Do you want to watch a movie with me?

régie f.   *state control, government control*
Cette entreprise a été mise en régie.
This company was put under state control.

régime m.   *regime, diet*
Il suit un régime pour perdre du poids.
He's on a diet to lose weight.

règle f.   *rule*
Les règles de sécurité sont faciles à suivre.
The safety regulations are easy to follow.

réglé(e)   *settled, in order*
Je suis heureuse de vous annoncer que toutes mes affaires sont
    réglées.
I am pleased to announced that all my affairs are in order.

regretter   *to regret, to feel sorry*
Ils regrettent que tu sois si triste.
They feel sorry that you are so sad.

reine f.   *queen*
Elle se déguise en reine pour la fête.
She's dressing up as a queen for the party.

rejeter   *to reject*
J'espère que notre candidat va rejeter cette loi.
I hope that our candidate will reject this law.

reluquer   *to eye*
Elle est si belle que je ne cesse pas de la reluquer.
She's so beautiful that I can't stop eyeing her.

remède m.   *remedy*
Je cherche un remède contre cette maladie.
I'm looking for a remedy for this illness.

remercier   *to thank*
Je vous remercie.
Thank you.

remettre   *to put back, to hand back, to hand over*
Elle m'a remis la lettre sans rien dire.
She handed me the letter without saying anything.

remplir   *to fill*
Elle a rempli le seau avec de l'eau.
She filled the bucket with water.

rencontre f.   *meeting, meet-up, encounter*
Elle nous parle de sa rencontre avec un cinéaste très connu.
She's telling us about her encounter with a very well-known film director.

rencontrer   *to meet*
J'ai rencontré beaucoup de collègues au congrès.
I met a lot of colleagues at the conference.

rendement m.   *output, yield, productivity*
Les cadres attendent avec impatience le rapport sur le rendement mensuel de leur entreprise.
The executives are patiently waiting for their company's monthly productivity report.

rendez-vous m.   *meeting*
Elle ne peut pas déjeuner avec nous parce qu'elle a un rendez-vous très important.
She can't have lunch with us because she has an important meeting.

rendre   *to give back, to render or make*
Le prof va rendre les rédactions demain.
The teacher is going to give back the compostions tomorrow.
Ça me rend heureux.
That makes me happy.

rendre compte, se   *to realize*
Je n'aime pas nos voisins; je m'en suis rendu compte hier quand j'ai vu tous les déchets qu'ils avaient laissé sur notre pelouse.
I dislike our neighbors; I realized this yesterday when I saw all the trash they left on our lawn.

rendre visite   *to visit someone*
Mes cousins vont nous rendre visite l'été prochain.
My cousins are going to visit us next summer.

renfrogné(e)   *sullen, sulky*
Pourquoi cette expression renfrognée?
Why this sullen expression?

renouer   *to get back in touch with*
L'année dernière j'ai renoué avec une copine du lycée et maintentant on se voit une fois par mois.
Last year I got back in touch with a girlfriend from high school, and now we see each other once a month.

renseigner   *to give information to someone*
J'ai besoin d'être renseigné sur les inconvenients de ce projet.
I need to be given information about the inconvenient aspects of this project.

rentable   *profitable*
Ce type de travail est très peu rentable.
This type of work is not very profitable.

repas m. *meal*
Comme elle est malade, elle prend ses repas au lit.
Since she's sick, she has her meals in bed.

repasser *to iron*
Tu dois acheter des vêtements qui sont faciles à repasser.
You should buy clothes that are easy to iron.

repère m. *marker, reference point*
Je cherche un repère pour m'orienter.
I am looking for a reference point so I can find my bearings.

répéter *to repeat*
Elle ne fait que répéter ce que les autres disent.
She only repeats what others say.

répondre *to answer, to respond*
Comment a-t-il répondu à ta question?
How did he answer your question?

réponse f. *answer, response*
Quelle est votre réponse?
What is your answer?

reposer, se *to rest, to relax*
Et si on se reposait avant la fête?
How about if we rest before the party?

résolu(e) *resolute, determined*
Elle est résolue à passer cet examen.
She's determined to pass this test.

respirer *to breathe*
Le yoga m'apprend à respirer.
Yoga teaches me to breathe.

resquilleur(-euse) *squatter, line jumper, queue jumper, fare dodger*
Le flic est à la recherche de ces resquilleurs qu'on avait vus à la station précédente.
The cop is looking for the fare dodgers we saw at the last station.

ressentir *to feel, to experience*
Elle ressent du bonheur en voyant son bébé lui sourire.
She feels happy when she sees her baby smile at her.

rester   *to stay*
Tu restes ici pendant combien de semaines?
How many weeks are you staying here?

résumer   *to sum up, to summarize*
Je vais résumer pour toi en un mot: viré!
I'm going to sum it up for you in one word: fired!

retard   *late*
Je me couche tard le soir.
I go to bed late at night.

retard, en   *late*
Ils arriveront en retard, comme toujours.
They'll arrive late, as usual.

retarder   *to make someone late*
La circulation m'a retardé.
The traffic made me late.

retirer   *to withdraw, to pull out*
Elle retire de l'argent de la banque pour payer ses factures.
She's withdrawing money from the bank to pay her bills.

retors(e)   *wicked, devious, crafty, perverse*
C'est un homme retors qui profite de toute situation.
He's a devious man who takes advantage of every situation.

retour m.   *return*
Votre retour est pour quand?
When are you returning?

retourner   *to return, to go back*
Nous pensons y retourner l'année prochaine.
We're thinking about going back next year.

retraite, prendre sa f.   *to retire*
Mon oncle prend sa retraite le printemps prochain.
My uncle is retiring next spring.

réussir   *to succeed, to pass (an exam)*
Votre fils est un étudiant brillant qui résusssira dans la vie.
Your son is a brilliant student who will succeed in life.

réunion f.   *meeting*
Notre réunion est pour 14h.
Our meeting is at 2 pm.

revanche f.   *revenge, vengeance*
Ne vous en faites pas, je prendrai ma revanche bientôt.
Don't worry, I'll take my revenge soon enough.

rêvasser   *to daydream, to muse*
Elle passe son temps à rêvasser et planifier sa vie.
She spends her days daydreaming and planning her life.

réveiller   *to wake someone up*
Elle réveille ses enfants pour qu'ils puissent se préparer pour l'école.
She wakes up her kids so they can get ready for school.

réveiller, se   *to wake up*
Normalement je me réveille vers sept heures du matin.
Normally I get up around seven a.m.

revendiquer   *to claim, to demand*
Je revendique mon droit de ne rien faire le dimanche!
I'm claiming my right to do nothing on Sundays!

revenir   *to come back*
Tu reviens quand?
When are you coming back?

rêver   *to dream*
Hier soir j'ai rêvé que je passais des vacances en Egypte.
Last night I dreamed that I was on vacation in Egypt.

revue f.   *magazine*
J'ai lu un très bon article dans cette revue.
I read a very good article in this magazine.

rhume m.   *cold*
J'ai un rhume depuis lundi.
I've had a cold since Monday.

riche   *riche*
Ce couple est riche mais a très mauvais goût.
This couple is rich but has very bad taste.

rien   *nothing*
Rien n'est impossible.
Nothing is impossible.

rigoler   *to have fun, to joke around*
On a bien rigolé dans le cours et on n'a rien appris.
We joked around in class, and we didn't learn anything.

rigueur f.   *strictness, harshness*
On est en train de vivre une période de rigueur financière dans
notre pays.
*We are in the midst of a period of financial strictness in our
country.*

ringard(e)   *out of fashion/style, no longer in style*
Tu vas porter cette robe ringarde à la fête?
Are you wearing this out-of-style dress to the party?

rire   *to laugh*
C'est un homme qui adore rire.
He's a man who loves to laugh.

risée f.   *laughingstock*
Après leur comportement puérile et honteux, l'équipe nationale
est la risée du monde.
*After their childish and shameful behavior, the national team is the
laughingstock of the world.*

robe f.   *dress*
Quelle jolie robe, tu l'as achetée où?
What a beautiful dress; where did you buy it?

rôder   *to prowl around, to lurk*
Il y a un chat sauvage qui rôde autour de notre maison la nuit.
There is a feral cat that prowls around our yard at night.

roi m.   *king*
Le roi vient de mourir. Vive la reine!
The king has died. Long live the queen!

rompre   *to break*
Il a décidé de rompre avec le passé.
He decided to break from the past.

ronchon   *grouchy, grumpy*
Notre prof de maths est toujours ronchon. Bref, c'est un homme
très désagréable.
*Our math teacher is always grumpy. Simply put, he's a very
disagreeable man.*

rondement   *promptly, frankly, briskly*
Elle nous a rondement critiqués pour notre paresse.
She briskly criticized us for our laziness.

ronfler   *to snore*
Je ne vais plus jamais partager une chambre d'hôtel avec ma
sœur parce qu'elle ronfle.
*I'm never sharing a hotel room again with my sister because she
snores.*

rose   *rose; pink*
Tu vas certainement voir Caroline dans la foule—elle porte une
robe rose avec des sandales orange.
*You are certainly going to spot Caroline in the crowd—she's wearing a
pink dress and orange sandals.*

rôti m.   *roast*
On va servir des légumes avec notre rôti.
We're going to serve vegetables with our roast.

roublard(e)   *crafty, cunning*
Attention, c'est un mec roublard!
Watch out, he's a crafty guy!

rouge   *red*
Il a brûlé le feu rouge et a eu une amende.
He ran a red light and got a ticket.

rougir   *to blush*
Tous ces compliments le font rougir.
All of these compliments are making him blush.

rouspéter   *to grumble, to complain*
On rouspète parce qu'ils ont supprimé notre train.
We're grumbling because they canceled our train.

route f.   *way, highway, road, route*
Connaissez-vous la route qui mène à cette ville?
Do you know the road that leads to this city?

royal(e)   *royal*
Il se dit de sang royal mais on ne le croit pas.
He says he's from a royal bloodline, but we don't believe him.

rue f.   *street*
Les enfants de ce quartier aiment jouer dans la rue.
Kids in this neighborhood like to play in the street.

rumeur f.   *rumor*
Ne fais pas attention à cette rumeur, c'est un mensonge.
Don't pay attention to this rumor: it's a lie.

rupin(e)   *(colloquial) swanky, loaded*
Elle ne fréquente que des gens rupins, ce que je trouve odieux.
She only hangs around people who are swanky, which I find disgusting.

rusé(e)   *cunning, crafty*
Dans ce conte de fée, il s'agit d'un renard rusé qui dupe un lapin innocent.
This fairy tale is about a cunning fox that tricks an innocent rabbit.

S

sable m.   *sand*
Le sable est si chaud qu'on n'arrive même pas à marcher dessus.
The sand is so hot that we can't even walk on it.

sac m.   *sack, bag*
Mets tes affaires dans ce sac en plastique.
Put your things in this plastic bag.

saccadé(e)   *jerky, clipped*
Il parle d'une voix saccadée.
He speaks in a clipped voice.

sacré(e)   *holy, sacred (colloquial) one hell of*
C'est un lieu sacré.
This is a holy place.
Quel sacré menteur!
He's one hell of a liar!

sain(e)   *healthy, sane*
Il essaie de suivre un régime plus sain.
He's trying to follow a healthier diet.

saisir   *to seize, to grab*
L'agent de police a saisi le cambrioleur pendant qu'il s'échappait de la maison.
The police officer caught the burglar while he was escaping from the house.

salade f.   *salad*
Elle nous a servi une salade niçoise délicieuse.
She served us a delicious Niçoise salad.

sale   *dirty*
Je refuse de monter dans sa voiture parce qu'elle est trop sale.
I refuse to ride in his car because it's too dirty.

salé(e) *salty*
J'adore les frites parce qu'elles sont salées.
I love French fries because they are salty.

salle à manger f. *dining room*
On va déjeuner dans la salle à manger.
We're going to have lunch in the dining room.

salle de bains f. *bathroom*
Elle a de l'eau de Javel pour nettoyer sa salle de bain.
She has some bleach for cleaning her bathroom.

salon m. *livingroom*
Prenons du thé dans le salon.
Let's have some tea in the livingroom.

saluer *to greet*
Il faut apprendre aux étudiants comment saluer les gens dans
d'autres pays.
It's necessary to teach students how to greet people in other countries.

salut *hi*
Salut Pierre! Salut Miriam, ça va?
Hi, Peter! Hi, Miriam! How are you?

sang m. *blood*
Il y a eu un accident dans la rue et il y a du sang partout.
There was an accident in the street, and there is blood everywhere.

sangloter *to sob*
Elle sanglotait pendant tout le film parce qu'elle l'a trouvé
triste.
*She was sobbing throughout the entire film because she found it
to be so sad.*

sans *without*
Je ne peux pas fonctionner sans café.
I can't function without coffee.

santé f. *health*
Elle est en bonne santé.
She's in good health.

saper *to undermine*
Alors, tu essaies de saper l'autorité de notre directeur, c'est ça?
*So, you're trying to undermine the authority of our director, is
that it?*

satisfait(e)   *satisfied*
L'architecte n'est pas du tout satisfait de son projet.
The architect isn't at all satisfied with her project.

sauce f.   *sauce, dressing*
Il faut mettre la sauce avant de servir les pâtes.
You have to put in the sauce before serving the pasta.

sauf   *except, but*
Il travaille tous les jours sauf le lundi.
He works every day but Monday.

saugrenu(e)   *crazy, absurd*
C'est une femme bizarre qui a des idées vraiment saugrenues.
She's a crazy woman with really absurd ideas.

sauter   *to jump; to leave out, skip*
Hier j'ai vu les mômes de mon quartier sauter à la corde, elles
   sont très talentueuses!
*Yesterday I saw the neighborhood kids jumping rope—they are really
   talented!*
Tu n'as pas besoin de lire tout ce document, saute jusqu'à la fin.
You don't need to read the whole document; skip to the end.

savoir   *to know*
Nous voudrions savoir si elle sait nager.
We would like to know if she can swim.

savoir-faire m.   *know-how*
Elle a peu de savoir-faire mais beaucoup d'enthousiasme.
She has little know-how but a lot of enthusiasm.

savon m.   *soap*
Elle fabrique du savon avec ses enfants.
She makes soap with her kids.

sciemment   *knowingly*
Elle l'a fait sciemment et sans hésitation.
She did it knowingly and without hesitation.

scier   *to saw; (colloquial) to stun, to bowl over*
Le menuisier scie.
The carpenter is sawing.
Tu nous as sciés avec ton histoire!
You bowled us over with your story!

scruter   *to examine, to scrutinize*
Le rédacteur scrute mon article avant de le faire imprimer.
The editor is scrutinizing my article before having it published.

se   *oneself*
Il se lave.
He's washing himself

sec(-èche)   *dry*
Je voudrais un martini sec.
I'd like a dry martini.

sécher   *to dry*
Tu devrais faire sécher ton maillot de bain au soleil.
You should dry your swimsuit in the sun.

second(e)   *second, second-rate*
C'est un hôtel de seconde classe.
It's a second-rate hotel.

secours m.   *help*
Au secours!
Help!

sein m.   *breast, bosom; heart of something*
J'ai choisi de nourrir mes jumeaux au sein.
I've decided to breastfeed my twins.
Au sein de ce mouvement politique, il y a une idéologie
    troublante.
At the heart of this political movement, there's a troubling ideology.

séisme m.   *earthquake*
Les séismes de cette amplitude sont très dangereux.
Earthquakes of this magnitude are very dangerous.

sel m.   *salt*
Mets du sel dans la sauce, elle est un peu fade.
Put some salt in the sauce; it's a bit bland.

selon   *according to*
Selon les experts, les changements s'effectueront tout de suite.
According to the experts, the changes will take place immediately.

semaine f.   *week*
On s'est vus la semaine dernière.
We saw each other last week.

semblable   *similar, identical*
Ces deux choses ne sont pas du tout semblables.
These two things are not at all similar.

sens m.   *sense, meaning; direction*
Quel est le sens littéral de ce mot?
What is the literal meaning of this word?
On va dans le mauvais sens, je crois. Donne-moi la carte.
We're going in the wrong direction, I think. Give me the map.

sentir   *to smell*
Ça sent mauvais!
That smells bad!

sentir, se   *to feel*
Je me sens heureux.
I feel happy.

séparer   *to separate*
Le maître doit séparer les élèves qui bavardent.
The schoolteacher needs to separate the students who chitchat.

sérieux (-ieuse)   *serious*
C'est une femme très sérieuse.
She's a very serious woman.

serveur (-euse) m. (f.)   *waiter / waitress*
Notre serveur est inepte, il a oublié notre commande deux fois.
Our waiter is inept; he forgot our order twice.

serviette f.   *towel, napkin*
Mets la serviette sur la table.
Put the napkin on the table.

servir   *to serve*
Je peux te servir quelque chose?
Can I serve you something?

seuil m.   *threshold, doorway*
Après trois ans, notre enterprise atteint enfin le seuil de rentabilité.
After three years, our company is finally attaining the threshold of profitability.

seul(e)   *alone*
Il vit seul avec ses quatre chiens.
He lives alone with his four dogs.

seulement   *only*
Il y a seulement trois trains par jour à destination de Paris donc on devrait réserver une place tout de suite.
There are only three trains a day to Paris, so we should reserve a seat right away.

shampooing m.   *shampoo*
Ce shampooing est très cher mais très efficace.
This shampoo is really expensive but works really well.

si   *if*
Si tu me donnes ta montre, je la réparerai.
If you give me your watch, I'll fix it.

si   *yes (affirmative answer to a negative question)*
Tu n'aimes pas Philippe? Si, il est très gentil!
You don't like Philip? Yes, he's very nice!

siècle m.   *century*
Elle étudie la musique du dix-neuvième siècle.
She is studying nineteenth-century music.

siffler   *to whistle, to blow a whistle; to hiss, to boo*
Je siffle en travaillant.
I whistle while I work.
L'assistance a commencé à siffler le musicien après seulement quelques minutes.
The audience started booing the musician after only a few minutes.

signal m.   *signal*
Attendez le signal avant de partir.
Wait for the signal before leaving.

signer   *to sign*
Pouvez-vous signer ici, s'il vout plaît?
Can you sign here, please?

simple   *simple*
Ce calcul est très simple.
This calculation is very simple.

sinon   *or else, otherwise*
Fais tes tâches ménagères sinon tu auras des ennuis avec ta mère.
Do your chores or else you'll have problems with your mother.

siroter   *to sip while savoring*
Il faut siroter ce cocktail pour vraiment l'apprécier.
You have to sip this cocktail to really appreciate it.

snob m.   *snob, snobbish*
Julie et Carole sont très snob, personne n'est à leur hauteur.
Julie and Carole are very snobbish; no one is good enough for them.

socle m.   *pedestal, foundation, base*
Ce concept est le véritable socle philosophique de notre société.
This concept is the veritable philosophical foundation of our society.

soie f.   *silk*
Elle portait une robe en soie magnifique.
She wore a magnificent silk dress.

soif, avoir f.   *to be thirsty*
Avez-vous soif?
Are you thirsty?

soigner, se   *to care for oneself*
Soigne-toi pour ne pas tomber malade.
Take care of yourself so you don't get sick.

soir m.   *night, evening*
Il fait assez chaud le soir dans cette région.
It's pretty warm in this region in the evenings.

soirée f.   *night, evening*
On a passé une soirée agréable avec nos amis.
We spent a pleasant evening with our friends.

soleil m.   *sun*
Le soleil brille très fort.
The sun is shining brightly.

sommeil, avoir m.   *to be sleepy*
Si tu as sommeil, couche-toi!
If you're sleepy, go to bed!

son (sa, ses) m. (f., pl.)   *hers/his*
J'aime son fils / sa fille / ses enfants.
I like his/her son / his/her daughter / his/her kids.

sorcier(-ière) m. (f.)   *witch, sorcerer*
Il se déguise en sorcière pour le bal masqué.
He's dressing up as a sorcerer for the masquerade ball.

souci m.   *problem, worry*
Il a beaucoup de soucis en ce moment avec son travail.
He has a lot of problems at work these days.

soucier, se . . . de   *to care about someone or something*
Elle ne se soucie de personne.
She doesn't care about anyone.

soudain   *sudden*
Son départ soudain nous a surpris.
His sudden departure surprised us.

soudainement   *suddenly*
On n'avait pas vu Eric pendant des mois et puis soudainement il
    nous a contacté.
We hadn't seen Eric for months and then suddenly he contacted us.

soudoyer   *to bribe*
On dit que cet homme a soudoyé la police pour qu'elle ferme
    l'œil sur ses affaires clandestines.
*People say that this man bribed the police so they would ignore his
    illegal dealings.*

souffrance f.   *suffering*
Elle a connu beaucoup de souffrances dans sa vie.
She's experienced a lot of suffering in her life.

souhait m.   *desire, wish*
Mon souhait le plus cher est de revoir mes amis en Irelande.
My fondest wish is to see my friends in Ireland again.

souhaiter   *to wish/hope for, to desire*
Il est à souhaiter que tout le monde accepte ces changements.
It is to be hoped that everyone will accept these changes.

soulager   *to relieve, to ease, to make someone feel better*
Ce médicament soulage les douleurs.
This medication relieves aches and pains.

soupçon m.   *suspicion, inkling; (colloquial) drop of, spot of*
Si j'ai le moindre soupçon que tu me mens, alors ce sera fini entre
    toi et moi.
If I have the slightest inkling that you are lying to me, then we are finished.
Donnez-moi un soupçon de vin, s'il vous plaît.
Give me drop of wine, please.

soupçonner   *to suspect*
Elle vous soupçonne d'être coupable.
She suspects that you are guilty.

souper m.   *dinner (Québec)*
Tu prends quoi comme souper?
What are you having for dinner?

souper   *to have dinner (Québec)*
Ce soir on va souper chez Caroline.
Tonight we're having dinner at Caroline's.

sourire   *to smile*
Elle sourit tout le temps.
She smiles all the time.

sournois(e)   *underhanded*
J'en ai marre de tes tours sournois!
I'm sick of your underhanded tricks!

sous   *under, beneath*
Si je ne suis pas là, glisse le contrat sous ma porte.
If I'm not there, slide the contract under my door.

soutenu(e)   *formal, sustained*
Le ton de cette lettre n'est pas assez soutenu.
The tone of this letter isn't formal enough.

soutien m.   *support*
Sans le soutien de mes parents, je n'aurais pas pu finir mes
    études.
*Without the support of my parents, I wouldn't have been able to
    complete my studies.*

souvenir, se (de)   *to remember*
Je me souviens de toi!
I remember you!

souvent   *frequent*
On dîne souvent dans ce restaurant, on y mange très bien.
We frequently have dinner in this restaurant—the food is really good.

spectacle m.   *show*
J'ai assisté à un spectacle hier soir qui était formidable.
I went to a show last night that was fantastic.

sport m.   *sport*
Ma fille fait beaucoup de sport, elle est très active.
My daughter does a lot of sports; she's quite active.

stade m.   *stadium*
On se verra devant le stade juste avant le début du match.
We'll meet in front of the stadium right before the game begins.

stationner   *to park*
Il est interdit de stationner devant cette porte.
Parking in front of this door is forbidden.

statue f.   *statue*
Cette statue antique te ressemble beaucoup.
This antique statue looks a lot like you.

stylo m.   *pen*
Le prof exige que ses élèves utilisent un stylo à encre.
The teacher requires that her students use a fountain pen.

subitement   *suddenly*
Il est mort subitement, on ne s'y attendait pas du tout.
He died suddenly; we weren't expecting it at all.

subvenir aux besoins de   *to provide for*
Il a des difficultés à subvenir aux besoins de sa famille.
He has trouble providing for his family.

succès m.   *success*
Le film dont il parle est un succès énorme en France.
The movie he's talking about is an enormous success in France.

sucre m.
Tu prends du sucre avec ton thé?
Do you take sugar with your tea?

sucré(e)   *sweet*
Je n'aime pas la confiture; c'est trop sucrée.
I don't like jam; it's too sweet.

suffire   *to be enough*
Ça suffit! Ne m'en parle plus!
That's enough! Don't talk to me about it any more!

suivant(e)   *next, following*
On prendra le train suivant.
We'll take the next train.

suivre   *to follow, to take (a course)*
Je ne peux pas suivre votre argument.
I can't follow your argument.
Elles suivent un cours d'allemand.
They're taking a German course.

sujet de, au   *about*
Il rédige un article au sujet de la violence à l'école.
He's writing an article about violence in schools.

super   *(colloquial) super*
Elle est super gentille avec tout le monde.
She's super nice with everyone.

supplier   *to beg, to implore*
Donne-moi tes billets pour le concert de Madonna, je t'en supplie!
Give me your Madonna concert tickets—I'm begging you!

supporter   *to stand*
Les bébés ne peuvent pas supporter les bruits violents.
Babies can't stand loud noises.

supprimer   *to cut, to eliminate*
On a peur qu'ils suppriment nos emplois.
We're afraid that they're cutting our jobs.

sur   *on*
Le stylo est sur la table, n'est-ce pas?
The pen is on the table, right?

sûr(e)   *sure, reliable, certain*
Je suis sûre que tu vas aimer cette chanson!
I'm sure you're going to love this song!

surmener   *to overwork*
Il a tendance à surmener ses employés, donc fais gaffe!
He has a tendancy to overwork his employees, so be careful!

surmonter   *to overcome*
Elle a surmonté pas mal d'obstacles pour arriver à ce point-là.
She overcame many obstacles to get to this point.

sursaut m.   *sudden burst, start*
Tu as un sursaut d'énérgie et tu veux ranger?
You're having a sudden burst of energy and you want to clean?

sursis m.   *reprieve, stay of execution*
Voilà ton sursis—ton prof est malade et tu n'auras pas d'épreuve
    aujourd'hui!
*Here's your reprieve—your teacher is sick and you won't have a test
    today!*

surtout   *above all*
J'aime bien le vin blanc mais j'aime surtout
    le vin rouge.
*I like white wine, but I like red wine
    above all.*

surveiller   *to put under surveillance, to watch, to supervise*
J'évite le sucre parce que je surveille mon poids.
I avoid sugar because I'm watching my weight.

susciter   *to spark, to give rise to, to elicit*
Votre lettre à la rédaction a suscité un grand débat chez les
    lecteurs de ce journal.
*Your letter to the editor sparked a big debate among the readers of this
    paper.*

susurrer   *to whisper*
Elle m'a susurré des mots que je ne peux répéter.
She whispered words to me that I cannot repeat.

sympathique   *nice*
Elle est toujours sympathique avec tout le monde.
She's always nice with everyone.

T

tabac m.   *tobacco, tobacco shop*
Je suis allergique à la fumée de tabac.
I'm allergic to tobacco smoke.
Je vais passer par le tabac pour acheter des
    allumettes.
*I'm going to stop by the tobacco shop to buy
    some matches.*

table f.   *table*
Mettons-nous à table.
Let's sit down at the table.

tableau(x) m. (pl.)   *picture, painting*
Cet après-midi on a vu des tableaux magnifiques.
This afternoon we saw some magnificent paintings.

tabler   *(colloquial) to bank on*
Je table sur l'arrivée du Beaujolais nouveau pour notre fête.
I'm banking on the arrival of the Beaujolais nouveau for our party.

tablier m.   *apron*
Mets ton tablier avant de faire ton gâteau.
Put your apron on before making your cake.

tabouret m.   *stool*
Les hommes étaient tous assis dans la cour sur des tabourets.
The men were all seated on stools in the courtyard.

taille f.   *size*
Il est de taille moyenne.
He's medium-sized.

tailler   *to trim, to sharpen, to shape*
Peux-tu tailler ma barbe?
Can you trim my beard?

talonner   *to pursue someone hotly, to follow on someone's heels*
On dit qu'elle talonne son ex-copain mais c'est une exagération.
*People say that she's in hot pursuit of her ex-boyfriend, but that's an
     exaggeration.*

tamis m.   *sieve*
Il faut passer la farine au tamis.
You must put the flour through the sieve.

taper   *to type; to hit*
Cette rédaction doit être tapée à la machine.
This composition should be typed.
Il a tapé son chien, quel idiot!
He hit his dog. What an idiot!

taquiner   *to tease, to joke with someone*
Tu me taquines, c'est ça?
So you're teasing me, is that it?

tarabiscoté(e)   *overly ornate, fussy, overly complicated*
Cette maison est un peu trop tarabiscotée pour nous.
This house is a bit too ornate for us.

tarabuster   *to pester, to bother*
A mon avis, tu dois l'éviter; elle nous tarabuste depuis un mois avec ses questions débiles.
In my opinion, you should avoid her; she's been pestering us with her stupid questions for a month.

tarder   *to take a long time doing something, to be slow at something*
Elle ne tarde pas à trouver un autre boulot.
She isn't taking a long time finding another job.

taré(e)   *(colloquial) crazy*
Elle est tarée, on ne comprend pas pourquoi il sort avec elle.
She's crazy—we don't understand why he's going out with her.

targuer, se   *to boast, to claim*
Il se targue de toutes ses capacités. Bof!
He boasts about all his abilities. Who cares!

tas m.   *a pile, load, heap*
On a vu un tas d'amis au café.
We saw loads of friends at the café.

tasse f.   *cup*
Voulez-vous une tasse de thé?
Would you like a cup of tea?

tâter, se   *to think about, to toy with*
Je me tâte pour aller à la fête.
I'm toying with the idea of going to the party.

taux m.   *level, rate*
Quel est le taux de change aujourd'hui?
What's the exchange rate today?

te   *you, to you*
Je t'aime.
I love you.
Il va t'écrire plus tard.
He's going to write to you later.

tel(le)   *such*
Un tel comportement va te causer des problèmes avec ton patron.
Such behavior is going to cause you problems with your boss.

télécharger   *to download*
Elles téléchargent des documents pour leur présentation cet après-midi.
They are downloading documents for their presentation this afternoon.

téléphone m.   *phone*
Je peux utiliser ton téléphone?
Can I use your phone?

téléphoner   *to call, to phone*
Il va nous téléphoner quand il aura fini.
He's going to call us when he's finished.

tellement   *so much, so*
Je suis tellement content de vous voir.
I'm so happy to see you.

téméraire   *reckless, rash*
Elle est très connue pour ses decisions téméraires.
She's well-known for her rash decisions.

témoigner   *to witness, to testify, to show*
Il témoigne d'un courage impressionant.
He shows impressive courage.

témoin m.   *witness*
Il n'y a pas de témoins à ton accident?
There are no witnesses to your accident?

tempête f.   *storm*
Les enfants espèrent que l'école sera fermer à cause de la tempête.
The kids are hoping that the school will close due to the storm.

temporiser   *to stall, to delay*
Tu temporises! Vas-y, à toi de jouer!
You're stalling! Go ahead, it's your turn!

temps m.   *time, weather*
Je n'ai pas le temps de te parler.
I don't have time to talk to you.
Quel temps fera-t-il demain?
What will the weather be tomorrow?

tendu(e)   *tense*
Notre réunion avec les membres du conseil était très tendue.
Our meeting with the members of the council was very tense.

teneur f.   *content, level*
Ce fruit a une très haute teneur en vitamines.
This fruit has a high vitamin content.

tenir   *to hold*
Tu dois me tenir la main quand on traverse cette rue.
You need to hold my hand when we cross this busy street.

tenter   *to try to do something, to attempt*
Elle tente de faire bonne impression sur sa belle-mère, mais ça ne
    marche pas.
*She's attempting to make a good impression on her mother-in-law, but
    it's not working.*

tenue f.   *attire, outfit; manners*
Cette tenue est tout à fait appropriée pour votre travail.
This outfit is completely appropriate for your job.
Un peu de tenue, Madame!
Watch your manners, Ma'am!

terre f.   *land, earth*
L'agriculteur a besoin de cultiver sa terre avant la prochaine saison.
The farmer needs to cultivate his land before the next season.

tête f.   *head*
Elle veut des comprimés parce qu'elle a mal à la tête.
She wants some pills because she has a headache.

têtu(e)   *stubborn*
Cet enfant têtu ne fait jamais ce que je lui dis de faire.
This stubborn kid nevers does what I tell him to do.

thé m.   *tea*
Et si on prenait une tasse de thé?
How about having a cup of tea?

théâtre f.   *theater*
Cette actrice talentueuse fait sa carrière entière dans le théâtre.
This talented actress is spending her entire career in the theater.

tiède   *lukewarm*
Mets de l'eau tiède dans la baignoire pour qu'elle puisse se baigner.
Put some lukewarm water in the bathtub so she can take a bath.

tiers m.   *third, third party*
Normalement on demande à un tiers de régler ce genre de situation.
Normally one asks a third party to take care of this type of situation.

tiers-monde m.   *Third World*
Il a écrit un livre au sujet des effets de la microfinance au
    tiers-monde.
He wrote a book about the effects of microfinance on the Third World.

timbre f.   *stamp*
Combien de timbres faut-il pour une lettre internationale?
How many stamps are needed for an international letter?

timide   *shy, timid*
Ne sois pas si timide! Dis ce que t'en penses!
Don't be so shy! Say what you think about it!

timoré(e)   *fearful, timid*
Elle est si timorée qu'elle n'ose pas parler à ses profs.
She is so timid that she doesn't dare speak to her teachers.

tiquer   *(colloquial) to bat an eye, to wince, to raise an eyebrow*
Eh bien, quand j'ai mentionné son divorce elle n'a pas tiqué.
Well, when I mentioned her divorce she didn't bat an eye.

tisane f.   *herbal tea*
Prenons une tisane pour nous calmer.
Let's have some herbal tea to calm down.

tissu m.   *fabric, material*
Il me faut du tissu pour la robe que je fais en ce moment.
I need fabric for the dress I'm making now.

tocard(e)   *(colloquial) trashy, cheap*
Je ne peux pas blairer son copain tocard.
I can't stand her cheap boyfriend.

toi   *you*
Elle est plus âgée que toi.
She's older than you.

toilette, faire sa f.   *to wash, to do one's daily hygiene routine*
Elle fait sa toilette avant de s'habiller.
She washes before getting dressed.

tollé m.   *outcry of indignation or protest*
Je comprends le tollé étant donné la manière dont ils ont annoncé
    la nouvelle.
I understand the outcry, given the way in which they announced the news.

tombée f.   *the fall, nightfall, the close of*
La tombée de la nuit est mon moment préféré de la journée.
Nightfall is my favorite time of the day.

tomber   *to fall*
L'enfant doit faire attention, sinon il va tomber.
The child needs to be careful or else he'll fall.

ton(ta, tes) m. (f., pl.)   *your*
J'aime ton pull / ta chemise / tes sabots.
I like your sweater / your shirt / your clogs.

ton m.   *tone*
Je n'apprécie pas le ton de ce message.
I don't appreciate the tone of this message.

tondre   *to shear, to clip, to mow*
J'ai demandé à mon neveu de tondre le gazon mais il a refusé—
quel moutard!
I asked my nephew to mow the lawn but he refused—what a brat!

tonus m.   *tone, energy, dynamism*
On aime bien travailler avec Jérôme parce qu'il donne toujours
du tonus.
*We like working with Jerome because he always brings some
energy.*

torpiller   *to torpedo, to sabotage*
Quelqu'un a torpillé mes projets pour ce soir, mais qui?
Someone sabotaged my plans for this evening, but who?

tôt   *early*
Couche-toi maintenant parce qu'on se lève tôt demain.
Go to bed because we're getting up early tomorrow.

toucher   *to touch, to reach, to affect*
Regardez, mais ne touchez pas à mes affaires!
Look, but don't touch my things!
Le tabagisme touche tout le monde.
Tobacco addiction affects everyone.

toujours   *always*
Elle a toujours un sourire pour ses étudiants.
She always has a smile for her students.

tour f. *tower*
La Tour Eiffel est une merveille architecturale.
The Eiffel Tower is an architectural marvel.

tour m. *tour, circuit, trick*
Je pense que le Tour de France est l'évènement sportif le plus
passionnant du monde.
*I think that the Tour de France is the most exciting sporting event
in the world.*

tourner *to turn*
Pour venir chez moi, continuez tout droit et puis tournez à gauche.
To come to my house, go straight and then turn left.

tournure f. *turn*
Quelle tournure d'évènements bizarre!
What a bizarre turn of events!

tout(es, tous) m. (f., pl.) *all, every*
Tous mes amis aiment bien le café mais moi je préfère le thé.
All my friends like coffee, but I prefer tea.

tous les deux *both*
Je les aime tous les deux.
I like both of them.

toux f. *cough*
Vous avez un sirop contre la toux?
Do you have cough syrup?

traduction f. *translation*
Quelle est la bonne traduction pour cette phrase?
What is the correct translation of this sentence?

traduire *to translate*
Pouvez-vous traduire ces mots?
Can you translate these words?

train m. *train*
Le train à destination de Nice sera en retard.
The train for Nice will be late.

traîner *to drag, to dawdle*
Ne traîne pas ta valise par terre, elle est trop chèr!
Don't drag your suitcase on the ground—it's very expensive!

traiteur m.   *caterer*
On doit engager un traiteur pour notre grande soirée.
We need to hire a caterer for our big party.

tranche f.   *slice, piece*
Donne-leur deux tranches de pizza.
Give them two slices of pizza.

tranquille   *calm, quiet, peaceful*
Je cherche un endroit tranquille dans la bibliothèque pour étudier.
I'm looking for a quiet place in the library to study.

travail m.   *work, job*
Elle cherche un travail parce que son enterprise va bientôt fermer.
She's looking for another job because her business is going to close soon.

travailler   *to work*
Les employées dans ce bureau détestent travailler le weekend.
The employees in this office hate working on weekends.

travers (à)   *through, across*
Elle voyage à travers le monde pour prendre des photos pour
    son livre.
She's traveling around the world to take pictures for her book.

traverser   *to cross*
Traverser l'Atlantique seul en bateau me semble très difficile.
Crossing the Atlantic alone in a boat seems very difficult to me.

trébucher   *to trip, to stumble*
Celui-là n'arrive pas à marcher sans trébucher.
That guys isn't able to walk without stumbling.

trembler   *to tremble, to shake*
Pendant les orages mon chien tremble beaucoup et on ne peut
    pas le calmer.
During storms my dog trembles a lot, and we can't calm him down.

tremper   *to soak, to dip*
Trempe ton biscuit dans ton thé, c'est délicieux comme ça.
Dip your cookie in your tea—it's delicious like that.

très   *very*
Après avoir fait du vélo dans cette chaleur il a très soif.
After biking in this heat he's really thirsty.

trêve f.   *truce, respite, recess*
Maintentant il y a une trêve entre mes enfants, espérons
que ça dure!
Now there is a truce between my children; let's hope it lasts!

tri, faire le m.   *to sort through*
Les ouvriers font le tri afin de trouver les déchets recyclables.
The workers are sorting the trash in order to find recyclables.

trimbaler   *to lug around, to drag around*
Il trimbale sa famille à tous les matchs de cette équipe.
He drags his family to every game of this team.

trinquer   *to clink glasses, to drink to something*
Alors trinquons à ton succès!
So let's drink to your success!

triste   *sad*
Elle sera triste quand tu lui diras les nouvelles.
She'll be sad when you tell her the news.

troc, faire du m.   *to barter*
Je n'aime pas faire du troc.
I don't like bartering.

tromper   *to cheat on someone, to deceive someone*
Il a trompé sa femme pendant dix ans.
He cheated on his wife for ten years.

tromper, se   *to be mistaken*
C'est notre PDG, si je ne me trompe pas.
That's our CEO, if I'm not mistaken.

tronche f.   *(colloquial) ugly mug*
Je n'aime pas du tout sa tronche!
I can't stand his ugly mug!

trop   *too much*
Elle a trop parlé.
She said too much.

trouer   *to make a hole, to wear out, to pierce*
Ma mère dit que mon père troue ses chemises si vite qu'elle a du
mal à les réparer.
*My mom says that my dad wears his shirts out so fast that she has a
hard time reparing them.*

trouille, avoir la f.   *(colloquial) to be scared*
Moi je ne veux pas y entrer, j'ai la trouille!
As for me, I don't want to go in there—I'm scared!

trouvaille f.   *find*
Tu as acheté une montre qui date des année 20 à la brocante?
     Quelle trouvaille!
You bought a watch from the 1920s at the flea market? What a find!

trouver   *to find*
Nous ne trouvons jamais son adresse avec notre GPS.
We never find his address with our GPS.

trouver, se   *to be located*
Où se trouve ta maison?
Where is your house located?

truc m.   *thing, thingamajig*
Il sert à quoi, ce truc?
What purpose does this thing serve?

trucmuche m.   *(colloquial) thingamajig*
J'ai trouvé ton trucmuche par terre et je l'ai mis sur la table.
I found your thingamajig on the floor and put it on the table.

tu   *you (informal)*
Tu as quel âge, jeune homme?
How old are you, young man?

turbin m.   *(colloquial) daily grind*
Ça va, ton turbin?
How's your daily grind going?

tutoyer   *to use "tu" with someone*
On se tutoie?
Shall we use "tu" with one another?

tuyau m.   *pipe; (colloquial) advice, tip*
Le tuyau est bloqué.
The pipe is blocked.
Elle dit qu'elle a un tuyau pour moi en ce qui concerne
     mon fric.
She says she has a tip for me about my money.

type m.   *(colloquial) guy*
Comment s'appelle le type dont on parlait toute à l'heure?
What's the name of that guy we were talking about?

typique   *typical*
Ça, c'est typique!
That's typical!

U

ulcérer   *to revolt, to sicken*
Les commentaires du politicien m'ulcèrent.
The politician's comments sicken me.

ultime   *last, final, ultimate*
L'ultime décision est la vôtre.
The final decision is yours.

un(e)   *one, a, an*
J'ai un frère / une sœur.
I have one brother / sister.

unique   *unique, only*
Barbara a acheté un livre unique.
Barbara bought a unique book.

université (f.)   *university*
Meredith était professeur à l'Université de Paris X–Nanterre.
Meredith was a professor at the University of Paris X–Nanterre.

untelle m. (f.)   *(colloquial) so-and-so, what's-his-name*
Tu as vu Untel au marché et tu n'as rien dit?
You saw what's-his-name at the market and you didn't say anything?

urgent(e)   *pressing, urgent*
Ce village a un besoin urgent de médecins.
This village has an urgent need for doctors.

urger   *to be urgent*
Tu dois compléter ce travail parce que ça urge.
You should complete this work because it's urgent.

user   *to wear out, to wear down*
Je ne veux plus porter ces sandales, elles sont trop usées.
I don't want to wear these sandals any more; they're too worn out.

usine f.   *factory*
Les ouvriers en grève manifestent devant leur usine.
The striking workers are protesting in front of their factory.

usité(e)   *used*
C'est une technique usitée par les artisans de cette région.
It's a technique used by the artisans of this region.

usuel(le)   *everyday, common*
Quel est l'emploi usuel de ce terme?
What is the common usage of this term?

utile   *useful*
Ce logiciel est très utile car il facilite certains calculs.
This software is very useful as it makes certain calculations easier.

utiliser   *to use*
Tu devrais utiliser cette crème hydratante pour ton visage.
You should use this moisturizer for your face.

V

vacances f. pl.   *vacation*
On a passé de très bonnes vacances en Tunisie l'année dernière.
We had a great vacation in Tunisia last year.

vacarme m.   *din, racket*
Je serai ravi de quitter tout le vacarme de ce quartier.
I will be thrilled to leave the racket of this neighborhood.

vacataire m.   *substitute teacher, replacement teacher*
Il n'a pas un poste contractuel; il est vacataire.
He doesn't have an employment contract; he's a substitute teacher.

vachard(e)   *nasty, mean*
On ne le supporte plus, il est trop vachard.
We can't stand him any more—he's too mean.

vache f.   *cow*
Il a peur d'attraper la maladie de la vache folle.
He's afraid of getting mad-cow disease.

vachement   *awfully, really (colloquial)*
Il est vachement sympa.
He's really nice.

vacherie f.   *nastiness, meanness, mean thing*
Elle fait tant de vacheries à ses amis.
She does plenty of mean things to her friends.

vaciller   *to falter, to quiver, to waiver*
Elle vacille entre le bonheur et la tristesse.
She waivers back and forth between happiness and sadness.

vadrouiller   *to wander around*
Quand elle voyage, elle aime vadrouiller dans les rues de
nouvelles villes.
When she travels, she likes to wander the streets of new towns.

vagabonder   *to wander, to roam*
Il passe sa vie à vagabonder entre Londres et Paris.
He spends his life wandering between London and Paris.

vague f.   *wave*
Lorsque le vent souffle sur la surface du lac, cela crée des vagues.
When the wind blows on the surface of the lake, it creates a series of waves.

valise f.   *suitcase*
Cette vielle valise n'est plus fonctionnelle.
This old suitcase is no longer usable.

vallée f.   *valley*
Pratiquement tous les produits laitiers de la région viennent de
cette vallée.
Almost all the dairy products from this region come from this valley.

valoir   *to be worth*
Ça vaut combien?
How much is that worth?

vanter   *to extol, to praise*
J'aimerais bien essayer ce café dont Pierre a tellement vanté les
qualités.
I'd like to try this coffee that Pierre praised so much.

vanter, se   *to boast about*
Il n'a pas de quoi se vanter.
He has nothing to boast about.

vaquer   *to attend to, to see to*
Tu devrais vaquer à tes occupations et me laisser tranquille.
You should attend to your own affairs and leave me alone.

vaseux(-euse)   *dazed, confused, out of it*
Il est tellement vaseux que l'on a du mal à le comprendre.
He's so dazed that we have a hard time understanding him.

vedette f.   *star*
Toutes les vedettes de Hollywood sont au Festival de Cannes
    pour promouvoir leurs films.
All the Hollywood stars are at the Cannes Film Festival to promote
    their movies.

veiller   *to keep watch over, to see to it*
Tu dois veiller à ce que les chiens restent dans la maison.
You need to see to it that the dogs stay in the house.

veilleuse f.   *night light*
Mets la veilleuse pour que le petit ne pleure pas la nuit.
Turn the night light on so that the little one doesn't cry at night.

veine, avoir de la f.   *to be lucky*
On lui a donné des billets pour le match ce soir, il a de la veine!
Someone gave him tickets to tonight's game—he's lucky!

veinard(e)   *lucky devil*
Mon prof a annulé le cours! Veinard!
My teacher canceled class! Lucky devil!

vélo m.   *bike*
On va lui donner l'ancien vélo de notre fils.
We're going to give him our son's old bike.

vélo, faire du m.   *to go bike riding*
On fera du vélo s'il fait beau demain.
We'll go bike riding tomorrow if it's nice.

vendeur(-euse) m. (f.)   *shopkeeper, salesman, saleswoman*
Le vendeur nous a donné un rabais.
The salesman gave us a discount price.

vendre   *to sell*
Je veux vendre ma maison.
I want to sell my house.

vénérer   *to venerate, to revere*
Les pèlerins viennent ici pour vénérer ce saint.
Pilgrims come here to venerate this saint.

venir   *to come*
Vous venez avec nous?
Are you coming with us?

vent m.   *wind*
Il y a du vent aujourd'hui.
It's windy today.

vérifier   *to check, to verify*
Le garagiste vérifie les pneus avant de nous donner notre voiture.
The mechanic is checking the tires before giving our car back to us.

véritable   *veritable, downright, genuine*
Vous êtes un véritable génie.
You are a veritable genius.

vérité f.   *truth*
Quelle est la vérité? On ne saura jamais.
What's the truth? We'll never know.

verre m.   *glass*
Vous voulez un verre de vin?
Do you want a glass of wine?
Cendrillon a porté une pantoufle de verre.
Cinderella wore a glass slipper.

vers   *toward, around*
Nous partons vers midi.
We're leaving around noon.

vert(e)   *green*
Tu devrais mettre une cravate verte avec ce costume noir.
You should wear a green tie with this black suit.

vertement   *strongly, pointedly, sharply*
Il vous a vertement répondu, n'est-ce pas?
He answered you sharply, didn't he?

vertige m.   *dizziness, vertigo*
Tout d'un coup, j'ai été pris de vertige donc je me suis vite assis.
I suddenly became quite dizzy, and so I quickly sat down.

veste f.   *jacket*
Cette veste en cuir est vraiment démodée!
This leather jacket is really out of style!

vexer   *to offend, to upset*
Je ne veux pas te vexer en disant cela, mais...
I don't want to upset you by saying this, but...

viager   *life annuity, for life*
Elle a cette maison en viager.
She has this house for life.

vide   *empty*
Le bocal est vide, il n'y a plus de confiture.
The jar is empty; there's no more jam.

vie f.   *life*
La vie est belle.
Life is beautiful.

vieux(vieille) (viel in front of a vowel and *h***)**   *old*
Je regrette le bon vieux temps!
I miss the good old days!
Ce vieil immeuble est trop délabré.
This old building is too dilapidated.
Cette une vieille amie de ma mère.
She's an old friend of my mother's.

village m.   *village*
Je déteste ce village morne.
I hate this dreary village.

ville f.   *city, town*
Quelle est la plus grande ville de cette région?
What is the biggest city in this region?

villégiature f.   *vacation, holiday*
On sera en villégiature en Grèce le mois prochain.
We'll be on vacation in Greece next month.

violet(te)   *purple*
Mon neveu porte toujours des baskets violettes, il les adore.
My nephew wears only purple tennis shoes; he loves them.

virer   *to fire*
Le PDG vient de virer toute l'équipe de marketing.
The CEO just fired the entire marketing team.

viser   *to aim at, to aim for, to target*
Je me sens vraiment visé par ses paroles.
I feel quite targeted by his words.

visser   *to screw on; (colloquial) to be glued to, to keep a tight rein on*
Il faut bien visser le couvercle sinon la boîte va s'ouvrir dans
   ton sac.
*You have to screw this lid on tight; if not the jar will open in
   your bag.*
On est vraiment vissé par notre patron, il nous surveille à tout
   moment.
*Our boss really keeps a tight rein on us—we are constantly being
   observed.*

vitesse f.   *speed*
Ce train roule à une très grande vitesse.
This train goes at a very high speed.

vivant(e)   *living, alive*
C'est incroyable mais après deux semaines sans eau nos plantes
   sont toujours vivantes.
*It's incredible, but after two weeks without water our plants are still
   alive.*

vivoter   *to struggle along*
Ce couple malheureux vivote depuis presque dix ans.
*This unhappy couple has been struggling along for almost
   ten years.*

vivre   *to live*
Elle rêve de vivre ailleurs, mais elle doit rester ici.
She dreams of living elsewhere, but she's stuck here.

voilà   *here is, there is, here you go*
Et voilà une raison de plus pour ne plus lui faire
   confiance.
And here is one more reason to no longer trust her.

voir   *to see*
Je veux voir le nouveau film de Scorsese, et toi?
I want to see Scorsese's new movie—how about you?

voire   *or even, not to say*
Le musicien est fatigué, voire malade.
The musician is tired, or even sick.

voisin(e) m. (f.)   *neighbors*
Les nouveaux voisins semblent assez gentils.
The new neighbors seem nice enough.

voiture f.   *car*
Quelle jolie voiture neuve, je suis jalouse.
What a beautiful new car—I'm jealous.

voix f.   *voice*
Elle a perdu la voix à force de tousser toute la nuit.
She lost her voice from coughing all night.

vol m.   *flight*
Leur vol part à minuit.
Their flight leaves at midnight.

volant m.   *steering wheel*
Il est strictement interdit d'envoyer des SMS pendant qu'on est
    au volant.
It's strictly forbidden to text while at the wheel.

voler   *to fly; to steal*
Les frères Wright rêvaient de voler.
The Wright brothers dreamed about flying.
Les cambrioleurs ont volé mes bijoux.
The burglars stole my jewels.

voleur (-euse) m. (f.)   *thief*
Voleur!
Thief!

volonté f.   *will*
Il est toujours plein de bonne volonté.
He's always full of good will.

volontiers   *gladly*
Tu viendras avec nous au lac? Volontiers!
You'll come with us to the lake? Gladly!

voter   *to vote*
Ma fille va voter pour la première fois cette année.
My daughter is going to vote for the first time this year.

vouloir   *to want, to desire*
Après trois heures de route, elle ne va pas vouloir s'asseoir à
    table pour trois heures de plus.
After three hours on the road, she's not going to want to sit down at the
    table for three more hours.

vouloir dire   *to mean*
Qu'est-ce que cela veut dire?
What does this mean?

vous   *you, to you*
Vous êtes américain, non?
You're American, right?
Je vous appelle plus tard.
I'm going to call you later.

vouvoyer   *to use "vous" (the polite "you")*
Quelle politesse! Tu n'as pas besoin de me vouvoyer!
Such politeness! You don't need to use "vous" with me!

voyage m.   *trip*
Elle n'est pas là; elle est en voyage.
She's not here; she's on a trip.

voyager   *to travel*
Moi, j'aime bien voyager mais mon mari préfère rester à la maison.
As for me, I like to travel, but my husband prefers to stay at home.

voyageur(-euse) m. (f.)   *traveler*
J'aurai aimé être un voyageur du temps!
I would have loved to be a time traveler!

voyou m.   *hood, delinquent, thug*
Ce quartier est plein de voyous.
This neighborhood is filled with delinquents.

voyoucratie f.   *thuggery, rule by thugs or criminals*
Le président parle souvent de l'importance de combattre la
    voyoucratie.
The president often speaks of the importance of fighting thuggery.

vrac, en m.   *in bulk, loose, unsorted*
Il faut acheter en vrac, c'est moins cher.
You should buy in bulk; it's less expensive.

vraiment   *really, truly*
Les joueurs sont vraiment fatigués après leur match de foot.
The players are really tired after their soccer game.

vue f.   *sight, view*
Elle a une bonne vue alors que moi, je dois porter des lunettes.
She has good eyesight, whereas I need to wear glasses.

vulgaire   *vulgar, coarse*
Je ne permets pas à mes enfants de regarder des films vulgaires.
I don't let my kids watch vulgar movies.

W

wagon-lit m.   *sleeper car*
Il a horreur de dormir dans le wagon-lit, il préfère piquer un
      roupillon dans son siège.
*He hates sleeping in the sleeper car; he prefers to snooze in
      his seat.*

X

xénophobe   *xenophobic*
Je déteste l'idéologie xenophobe de ce candidat.
I despise the xenophobic ideology of this candidate.

Xérès m.   *sherry*
Je peux vous offrir un verre de Xérès?
May I offer you a glass of sherry?

Y

y   *there, it*
Tu pars en Espagne? Oui, j'y vais tout de suite.
Are you leaving for Spain? Yes, I'm going there right away.
Je m'y attendais.
I was expecting it.

yaourt m.   *yogurt*
Elle refuse de manger le yaourt.
She refuses to eat the yogurt.

yeux m. pl.   *eyes*
J'ai mal aux yeux à cause de mes allergies.
My eyes hurt because of my allergies.

Z

zapper   *to channel surf*
On a passé tout le weekend à zapper et à ne rien faire.
We spent the whole weekend channel surfing and doing nothing.

zinzin   *crazy, nutty*
Il est un peu zinzin, non?
He's a little crazy, right?

zizanie f.   *discord, ill-feeling, feud*
C'est la zizanie entre ces deux familles depuis presque cinquante ans.
There has been a feud between these two families for almost fifty years.

zone f.   *area, zone*
Cette zone est interdite aux étudiants.
This area is off-limits to students.

zoo m.   *zoo*
On va au zoo cet après-midi, tu viens avec nous?
We're going to the zoo this afternoon—are you coming with us?

zouave m.   *clown, fool*
Pourquoi tu fais toujours le zouave?
Why do you always act like a clown?

Category Section

La Famille	The Family
beau-frère	brother-in-law
belle-sœur	sister-in-law
beau-père	father-in-law; stepfather
belle-mère	mother-in-law; stepmother
beau-fils	son-in-law; stepson
belle-fille	daughter-in-law; step-daughter
compagnon m.	partner, companion
copain	boyfriend
copine	girlfriend
conjoint(e)	spouse
cousin(e)	cousin
demi-frère	half-brother
demi-sœur	half-sister
femme	wife
fille	daughter
fils	son
frère	brother
grand-mère	grandmother
grand-père	grandfather
mari	husband
mère	mother
neveu	nephew

nièce	niece
oncle	uncle
partenaire m. / f.	partner
père	father
petits-enfants	grandchildren
petit-fils	grandson
petite-fille	granddaughter
sœur	sister
tante	aunt

Les Jours de la semaine	**Days of the Week**
lundi m.	Monday
mardi m.	Tuesday
mercredi m.	Wednesday
jeudi m.	Thursday
vendredi m.	Friday
samedi m.	Saturday
dimanche m.	Sunday

Les Mois	**Months of the Year**
janvier m.	January
février m.	February
mars m.	March
avril m.	April
mai m.	May
juin m.	June
juillet m.	July
août m.	August
septembre m.	September
octobre m.	October
novembre m.	November
décembre m.	December

| **Les Saisons** | **The Seasons** |
| printemps m. | spring |

été m.		summer	
automne m.		fall	
hiver m.		winter	

Les Nombres	Numbers	Les Nombres	Numbers
zero	0	dix	10
un	1	onze	11
deux	2	douze	12
trois	3	treize	13
quatre	4	quatorze	14
cinq	5	quinze	15
six	6	seize	16
sept	7	dix-sept	17
huit	8	dix-huit	18
neuf	9	dix-neuf	19
vingt	20	soixante	60
vingt et un	21	soixante-dix/ septante (Swiss)	70
vingt-deux	22	quatre-vingts/ huitante (Swiss)	80
vingt-trois	23	quatre-vingts-dix/ nonante (Swiss)	90
vingt-quatre	24	cent	100
vingt-cinq	25	cent un	101
vingt-six	26	deux cents	200
vingt-sept	27	trois cents	300
vingt-huit	28	cinq cents	500
vingt-neuf	29	mille	1 000
trente	30	deux mille	2 000
trente et un	31	vingt mille	20 000
quarante	40	cent mille	100 000
cinquante	50	un million	1 000 000

L'Heure	Telling Time
Il est dix heures.	It's ten a.m.
Il est trois heures et demi.	It's half past three.

Il est vingt-deux heures.	It's ten p.m.
Il est quatre heures moins le quart.	It's three forty-five.
Il est midi.	It's noon.
Il est deux heures et quart.	It's two-fifteen.
Il est minuit.	It's midnight.

Les Couleurs	Colors	Les Couleurs	Colors
la couleur	color	le noir	black
le blanc	white	l'orange	orange
le bleu	blue	le pourpre	purple
le brun	brown	le rose	pink
le gris	gray	le rouge	red
le jaune	yellow	le vert	green
le marron	chestnut	le violet	violet

La Nourriture	Food	La Nourriture	Food
abricot m.	apricot	boeuf m.	beef
agneau m.	lamb	bouillabaisse f.	fish soup
amande f.	almond	bouillon m.	broth
ananas m.	pineapple	café m.	coffee
anchois m.	anchovy	café-crème m.	coffee with hot milk
aperitif m.	before-dinner drink	canard m.	duck
artichaut m.	artichoke	carotte f.	carrot
aubergine f.	eggplant	cassis m.	blackcurrant
avocat m.	avocado	céleri m.	celery
baguette f.	French bread	cerise f.	cherry
beignet m.	fritter	champignon m.	mushroom
beurre m.	butter	châtaigne f.	chestnut
bière f.	beer	chou m.	cabbage
bifteck m.	steak	chou-fleur m.	cauliflower
biscuit m.	cookie	citrouille f.	pumpkin
concombre m.	cucumber	framboise f.	raspberry

confiture f.	jam	fromage m.	cheese
crustacés m. pl.	shellfish	fruit m.	fruit
cornichon m.	gherkin	fruits des bois m. pl.	berries
côtelette f.	cutlet	gâteau m.	cake
couscous aux légumes m.	vegetable couscous	glace f.	ice cream
		hamburger m.	hamburger
crème f.	cream	jambon m.	ham
crème caramel f.	caramel custard	jus m.	juice
crème chantilly f.	whipped cream	lait m.	milk
crevettes f. pl.	shrimp	laitue f.	lettuce
croissant m.	crescent roll	lapin m.	rabbit
croque-monsieur m.	hot ham-and-cheese sandwich	lard m.	bacon, fat
		haricots m. pl.	beans
dessert m.	dessert	haricots verts m. pl.	green beans
digestif m.	after-dinner liqueur	homard m.	lobster
dinde f.	turkey	huile f.	oil
eau f.	water	huître f.	oyster
épinards m. pl.	spinach	légume m.	vegetable
figue f.	fig	lentille f.	lentil
foie m.	liver	limonade f.	lemonade
fraise f.	strawberry	maïs m.	corn
melon m.	melon	poireau m.	leek
merlu m.	hake	pois, petits m. pl.	peas
miel m.	honey	pomme f.	apple
morue f.	cod	pomme de terre f.	potato
moutarde f.	mustard	poisson m.	fish
mouton m.	mutton	poivre m.	pepper
navet m.	turnip	poivron vert m.	green pepper
noix f.	nuts, walnut	porc m.	pork

noix de coco f.	coconut	potage m.	soup
nouilles f. pl.	noodles	poulet m.	chicken
œuf m.	egg	prune f.	plum
oignon m.	onion	radis m.	radish
olive f.	olive	raisin m.	grape
omelette f.	omelet	raisin sec m.	raisin
orange f.	orange	riz m.	rice
pain m.	bread	salade f.	lettuce, salad
pain grillé m.	toast	sandwich m.	sandwich
palourde f.	clam	sauce f.	sauce
pamplemousse f.	grapefruit	saucisse f.	sausage
pastèque f.	watermelon	saucisson m.	salami
pâtes f. pl.	pasta	sel m.	salt
pâtisserie f.	pastry	sorbet m.	sherbet
pêche f.	peach	sucre m.	sugar
petit pain m.	roll	tarte f.	pie
poire f.	pear	thé m.	tea
thon m.	tuna	viande f.	red meat
tomate f.	tomato	vin m.	wine
truite f.	trout	vinaigre m.	vinegar
veau m.	veal	yaourt m.	yogurt

Les Magasins	Shopping	Les Magasins	Shopping
bijouterie f.	jewelry store	magasin d'appareils-photo m.	camera store
blanchisserie f.	laundry	magasin de chaussures m.	shoe store
bureau de tabac m.	tobacco store	pâtisserie f.	pastry shop
boucherie f.	butcher's shop	pharmacie f.	pharmacy
boulangerie f.	bakery	poissonerie f.	fish shop
charcuterie f.	delicatessen	pressing m.	dry-cleaner
coiffeur, chez le m.	beauty salon, barber	quincaillerie f.	hardware store

grand magasin m.	department store	supermarché m.	supermarket
librairie f.	bookstore	traiteur, chez le m.	take-out place

Les Métiers	Occupations	Les Métiers	Occupations
architecte m. / f.	architect	banquier (-ière)	banker
artiste m. / f.	artist	boucher (-ère)	butcher
avocat(e)	attorney	boulanger (-ère)	baker
cadre m. / f.	executive	ouvrier (-ière)	worker/laborer
coiffeur (-euse)	barber, hair stylist	pâtissier (-ière)	pastry maker
comptable m. / f.	accountant	pharmacien (-ienne)	pharmacist
dentiste m. / f.	dentist	physicien (-ienne)	physicist
fonctionnaire m. / f.	govmt. employee	psychologue m. / f.	psychologist
infirmier (-ière)	nurse	secrétaire m. / f.	secretary
ingénieur (e)	engineer	sociologue m. / f.	sociologist
médecin m. / f.	doctor	tailleur m.	tailor
menuisier (-ière)	carpenter	vendeur (-euse)	salesperson

Les Ordinateurs et l'Internet		Computers and the Internet	
clavier m.	keyboard	lecteur MP3 m.	MP3 player
clé USB f.	flash drive	mèl m.	email
courriel m.	email	mot de passe m.	password
disque dur externe m.	external hard drive	navigateur m.	browser
données f. pl.	data	ordinateur m.	computer
envoyer un texto m.	to send a text message	ordinateur portable m.	laptop

fichier m.	file	portable m.	cellphone
imprimante f.	printer	souris f.	mouse
l'Internet	the Internet	SMS m.	text message
jeux video m.	pl. video games	télécharger	to download

La Communica-tion et les medias	Communica-tion and the Media	La Communi-cation et les medias	Communica-tion and the Media
abonnement m.	subscription	journal télévisé m.	TV news
actualités f. pl.	news	lecteur de DVD m.	DVD player
actualité f.	current affairs	magnéto-phone m.	tape recorder
médias m. pl.	the media	magnétoscope m.	VCR
câble m.	cable TV	publicité f.	advertisement
chaîne f.	channel	radio f.	radio
chaîne pub-lique f.	public station	revue f.	magazine
envoyé(e) spécial(e)	special reporter	télé f.	TV
émission f.	program	téléviseur m.	television set
journal m.	newspaper	télévision f.	television

Les Animaux	Animals	Les Animaux	Animals
aigle m.	eagle	oiseau m.	bird
chat m.	cat	ours m.	bear
cheval m.	horse	pigeon m.	pigeon
chèvre m.	goat	renard m.	fox
chien m.	dog	singe m.	monkey
grenouille f.	frog	souris f.	mouse
lion m.	lion	tigre m.	tiger
loup m.	wolf	tortue f.	turtle
mouton m.	sheep	vache f.	cow

Vocabulary Tips and *Faux Amis*

Because the English language has incorporated so many French words—with French words entering the English lexicon beginning with the Norman conquests in 1066 and subsequently continuing to be incorporated during the following centuries—English-speaking learners of French have an advantage when it comes to recognizing many words.

1. Examples of words that are spelled the same way in both languages:

| monument | six | prudent | variable | probable |
| rose | situation | client | principal | tropical |

2. Many *–er* verbs add a final *–r* to the English verb:

| amuser | comparer | encourager | guider | placer |
| admirer | continuer | dîner | obliger | voyager |

3. The English ending *–y* frequently corresponds to the French *–é*, *–ie*, or *–i*:

anxiété	beauté	fertilité	liberté	responsabilité
annuité	mélancolie	cérémonie	pharmacie	anatomie
photographie	essai	emploi	délai	convoi

4. English *–al* often corresponds to French *–el* / *–elle*

| annuel | éternel | intellectuel | maternel | officiel |

5. In many cases, the English *–oun* corresponds to the French *–on*:

| profond | fontaine | prononcer | renoncer | contenance |

6. The English *–ous* frequently becomes *–eux* / *–euse* in its French counterpart:

| curieux | dangereux | généreux | joyeux | malicieux |

7. In many French words containing *–ê*, *-ô*, adding an *–s* after the *accent circonflexe* will reveal the English word:

| honnête | fête | bête | hôtel | hôte |

Faux Amis

While there are many words common to both French and English, many others appear to mean the same thing in both languages, but, in fact, do not. These cognates, or *faux amis,* can be quite irksome! Here is a short list of the most commonly encountered offenders:

actuellement: currently, at the moment, **not** actually, in point of fact (véritablement)

assister: to witness, to attend, **not** to help (aider)

attendre: to wait for, **not** to show up for or attend (assister)

blesser: to wound, **not** to bless (bénir)

caractère: character or temperment, **not** character in a play (personnage)

chagrin : sorrow, grief, **not** distress, annoyance (agacement)

chair: flesh, **not** a seat, place one sits (siège, fauteuil)

chance: luck, **not** opportunity (occasion)

collège: junior high school, middle school, **not** university (l'université, la fac)

commander: to order something in a restaurant or a retail transaction, **not** to order a person to do something (ordonner)

compréhensif: to be understanding, **not** full or complete (complet)

contrôler: to check documents such as a passport, **not** to dominate (dominer, maîtriser)

crayon: pencil, **not** crayon (crayon à la cire)

demander: to ask for, **not** to demand (exiger)

douche: a shower, **not** a method of maintaining feminine hygiene

éducation: the way a child is brought up, **not** formal schooling (formation)

excité(e): sexually excited, **not** excitement in a general sense (animé, enthousiaste)

fastidieux: tedious, irksome, **not** meticulous (pointilleux)

figure: face, **not** famous individual (personne célèbre) or number (chiffre)

formidable: fantastic, amazing, **not** fear-inducing, difficult (redoutable)

ignorer: to not know something, to be unaware, **not** to purposely not pay attention to something or someone (ne pas prêter attention à) lecture: a reading, **not** a presentation in a scholarly setting (conférence)

librairie: a bookstore, **not** a library (bibliothèque)

location: the act of renting something, **not** a place (endroit)

opportunité: advisability or financial possibility, **not** chance at doing something (occasion)

patron: a boss, **not** a client (client)

place: a square in a town **not** a location (endroit)

publicité: an advertisement, **not** publicity (l'attention des medias)

réaliser: to fulfill an aspiration or achieve something, to finish a project, **not** to become aware of (se rendre compte)

rester: to stay or remain, **not** to get some rest (se reposer)
siège: a seat, a place to sit, **not** under siege (assiégé)

French Grammar Primer

Subject Pronouns

Je (I)	Nous (We)
Tu (You—informal sing.)	Vous (You—formal sing., pl. and informal pl.)
Il, Elle, On (He, She, One, We, It)	Ils, Elles (They—plural)

Note: You will frequently hear French speakers using "on" rather than "nous" for "we."

French Verbs

There are five categories of verbs in French: verbs with the endings -er, -re, -ir; stem-changing –er verbs; and irregular verbs. Conjugations for each type of verb, lists of verbs in each category, and sample sentences for the verbs are listed below.

–er verbs:

Verbs that follow the –er conjugation are done so by removing the –er from the infinitive and then adding the highlighted endings you see below.

Parler: to speak

je parl**e** (I speak)	nous parl**ons** (we speak)
tu parl**es** (you speak)	vous parl**ez** (you speak)
il/elle/on parl**e** (he/she/it speaks)	il/elles parl**ent** (they speak)

Common –er verbs

aimer	écouter	présenter
chanter	étudier	regarder
chercher	habiter	rester
danser	jouer	téléphoner
demander	marcher	travailler
donner	montrer	visiter

Sample sentences

Je ne parle que le français mais mes enfants parlent l'espagnol et le grec aussi.
J'aime mes amis parce qu'ils me téléphonent chaque jour.
Vous visitez Paris demain? Non, demain on visite Chartres.

Stem-changing –er verbs

Note that there is a subset of –er verbs that are called stem-changing or boot verbs, the latter name coming from the fact that when you take away the *nous* and *vous* conjugations (which have the same stem), you are left with the shape of a boot. Below is a chart showing you several common stem-changing verbs that you should be aware of:

Infinitive	1st person singular 2nd person singular 3rd person sing., pl.	1st person plural 2nd person plural	Examples
payer	-ie, -ies, -ie, -ient	-yons, -yez	je paie, nous payons

nettoyer	-ie, -ies, -ie, -ient	-yons, -yez	tu nettoies, vous nettoyez
jeter	-tte, -ttes, -tte, -ttent	–tons, -tez	elle jette, vous jetez
appeller	-lle, -lles, -lle, -llent	-lons, -lez	il appelle, nous appelons
célébrer	-èbre, - èbres, -èbre, -èbrent	-ébrons, -ébrez	je célèbre, nous célébrons
peser	-èse, -èses, -èse, -èsent	-ons, -ez	tu pèses, vous pesez

–ir verbs

Verbs that follow the regular –ir conjugation are done so by removing the –ir from the infinitive and then adding the highlighted endings you see below

Finir: to finish

je finis (I finish)	nous finissons (we finish)
tu finis (you finish)	vous finissez (you finish)
il/elle/on finit (he/she/it finishes)	il/elles finissent (they finish)

Common –ir verbs

choisir	maigrir	réfléchir
établir	mincir	réunir
grandir	obéir	réussir
grossir	réagir	vieillir

Sample Sentences

Mon fils m'obéit mais mes filles ne m'obéissent jamais.
Fatima maigrit alors que nous grossissons.
Tu ne vieillis pas!

–*re verbs*

Verbs that follow the regular –re conjugation are done so by removing the –re from the infinitive and then adding the highlighted endings you see below

Descendre: to go down

je descend**s** (I go down)	nous descend**ons** (we go down)
tu descend**s** (you go down)	vous descend**ez** (you go down)
il/elle/on descend (he/she/it goes down)	il/elles descend**ent** (they go down)

Common –re verbs

attendre	perdre
entendre	rendre
pendre	répondre

Sample Sentences

Ils perdent le match.
Elle rend visite à ses parents mais nous attendons la fin du mois pour voir les nôtres.
Tu m'entends? Oui, mais je ne te réponds pas.

Irregular Verbs

The following high-frequency verbs are all irregular verbs, meaning that they do not share a conjugation pattern with other verbs.

Avoir: to have

j'ai (I have)	nous avons (we have)
tu as (you have)	vous avez (you have)
il/elle/on a (he, she, one, it has)	ils/elles ont (they have)

Sample sentences

Nous avons un fils qui a 21 ans et des jumelles qui ont 14 ans.
Tu as un chien? Moi, non. J'ai une tortue.
Vous avez une jolie maison, Madame.

Être: to be

je suis (I am)	nous sommes (we are)
tu es (you are)	vous êtes (you are)
il/elle/on est (he, she, one is)	ils/elles sont (they are)

Sample sentences

Je suis Québecois mais mes cousins sont Algériens.
Tu es plus sympa que ton frère, qui est très méchant.
Vous êtes profs? Non, nous sommes architectes.

Faire: to do, to make

je fais (I do)	nous faisons (we do)
tu fais (you do)	vous faites (you do)
il/elle/on fait (he, she, one, it does)	ils/elles font (they do)

Sample sentences

Pourquoi tu fais tellement d'erreurs alors que Jean n'en fait jamais une seule?
On fait une tarte à la crème pour la soirée. Et vous, vous faites quoi?
Juliette fait du vélo pendant que ses enfants font la lessive.

Aller: to go

je vais (I go)	nous allons (we go)
tu vas (you go)	vous allez (you go)
il/elle/on va (he, she, one, it goes)	ils/elles vont (they go)

Sample sentences

Elias va en Espagne pendant que ses amis vont en Grèce.
Je vais aller en ville.
Nous allons à Paris.

Prepositions

A preposition is a word that establishes a relationship between different parts of a sentence, between nouns, or between a verb and a noun. Prepositions are placed before a noun and indicate a spatial or temporal meaning. Note that the forms of prepositions are fixed except for *à* and *de*, which combine with the definite articles *le, la,* and *les*:

à	at, to	*Maxime et Nicolas vont à Paris pour la Marche des Fiertés LGBT.* Maxime and Nicolas are going to Paris for the Gay Pride march.
à + le = au		*Je vais au stade.* I'm going to the stadium.
à + la = à la		*Ils travaillent à la bibliothèque depuis des années.* They've worked at the library for years.
à + les = aux		*Elles voyagent aux Seychelles pendant trois semaines.* They are traveling to the Seychelles for three weeks.
de	from, of about	*Vladimir est de Moscou.* Vladimir is from Moscow.
de + le = du		*On parle des problèmes économiques du pays.* We're talking about the country's economic problems.
de + la = de la		*On a vu la nouvelle voiture de la voisine.* We saw the neighbor's new car (car of the neighbor).

de + les = des   *Voilà le chat des enfants d'à côté.*
                              Here is the cat of the kids next door.

Below you will find a list of commonly used French prepositions, along with sample sentences that illustrate their usage.

à cause de	because, as a result of	*Ils ferment la fenêtre à cause du bruits de la rue.* They're closing the window because of the street noise.
à côté de	beside, next to	*Je peux m'asseoir à côté de vous?* May I sit next to you?
après	after	*Après le film, on va prendre un verre ensemble.* After the film, we're going to have a drink together.
à travers	through, across	*Elle voyage à travers le pays à vélo.* She's traveling across the country by bike.
au milieu de	in the middle	*On est vraiment au mileu de nulle part ici!* We're really out in the middle of nowhere here!
autour de	around	*Elle est contente avec ses amis autour d'elle.* She is happy with her friends around her.
avant	before	*Je te verrai avant la fin du mois?* Will I see you before the end of the month?
avec	with	*Tu prends du café ou du thé avec ce croissant?* Are you having coffee or tea with this croissant?
chez	at the place or house of	*On va chez Hélène ce soir.* We're going to Hélène's place tonight.
contre	against	*Ils sont contre les idées proposées par le conseil.* They are against the ideas proposed by the board.

dans	in	*On est tous dans le même bain!* We're all in the same boat!
derrière	behind	*Qu'est-ce qui est derrière cette porte?* What is behind this door?
devant	in front of	*On se voit devant le café à midi?* We'll meet each other in front of the café at noon?
en	in	*Malika étudie en Italie depuis deux ans.* Malika has been studying in Italy for two years.
en face de	in front of, across from	*Tu habites en face de la gare routière?* You live across from the bus station?
entre	between	*Entre toi et moi, je déteste la cuisine de Pierre.* Between you and me, I hate Peter's cooking.
envers	toward (figuratively)	*J'ai beaucoup d'animosité envers lui.* I have a lot of animosity toward him.
grâce à	thanks to	*Grâce à des contributions financières, le centre culturel restera ouvert.* Thanks to financial contributions, the cultural center will stay open.
jusqu'à	up to, as far	*J'irai jusqu'à Tours et puis je m'arrêterai dans un hôtel.* I'll go as far as Tours, and then I'll stop at a hotel.
loin de	far from	*Elle habite loin d'eux.* She lives far from them.
malgré	in spite of	*Malgré tous nos empêchements, on a pu déménager.* In spite of all our unforeseen difficulties, we were able to move.

par	by, per, through	*Envoyons cette lettre par avion.* Let's send this letter by air mail.
parmi	among amongst	*Il y a un traître parmi vous!* There is a traitor among you!
pendant	during, while	*Elle a travaillé à la Bourse pendant vingt ans.* She worked at the Stock Exchange for twenty years.
pour	for, in favor of	*Un cadeau, pour moi?* A present for me?
sans	without	*Ils travaillent ici sans papiers.* They're working here without papers.
sauf	except	*Le musée est ouvert tous les jours sauf le lundi.* The museum is open every day except Mondays.
selon	according to	*Selon Paul, personne ne veut travailler demain.* According to Paul, nobody wants to work tomorrow.
sous	under	*Les chattons se cachent sous le lit.* The kittens are hiding under the bed.
sur	on, on top of	*Mettez ce plat sur la table.* Put this plate on the table.
vers	toward, around (temporal, spatial sense)	*Appellez-moi vers midi!* Call me around noon!

Question Formation

There are four ways to form yes/no questions in French. These four ways have slight differences in the level of formality and register; they are listed below from most to least formal:

Inversion: This question formation inverts the subject pronoun and verb.

> Avez-vous des frères?
> *Do you have any brothers?*

> Que sais-je?
> *What do I know?*

Est-ce que: This question is formed by placing "est-ce que" in front of the subject-verb phrase.

> Est-ce que vous travaillez maintenant?
> *Are you working now?*

> Est-ce qu'ils habitent en ville?
> *Do they live in town?*

N'est-ce pas: In this form, *n'est-ce pas* is a tag question that is placed at the end of a sentence, eliciting a confirmation or denial.

> Tu sors avec Caro, n'est-ce pas?
> *You're going out with Caro, aren't you/right?*

> Tu parles grec, n'est-ce pas?
> *You speak Greek, don't you/right?*

Rising Intonation: You can transform any declarative sentence into an interrogative one by using a rising intonation at the end of the sentence.

> Tu viens?
> *Are you coming?*

> Tu n'as plus d'argent?
> *You don't have any more money?*

Negation

Making an affirmative sentence negative in French is usually achieved by inserting two words. Below your will find a chart of the most commonly used negations in French:

ne ... pas   **not**

J'aime les fruits mais je ne mange pas de bananes.
I like fruit but I don't eat bananas.

Je n'écoute pas!
I'm not listening!
[Note: ne in front of a vowel becomes n']

ne ... plus   **any more**

Elles n'ont plus d'argent.
They don't have any more money.

Tu ne fumes plus?
You no longer smoke?

ne ... jamais   **never**

Jean-Paul ne me parle jamais.
Jean-Paul never talks to me.

Ma mère n'a jamais visité Montréal.
My mom has never visited Montréal.

ne ... aucun(e)   **not any**

Elle n'a aucune confiance en moi.
She doesn't have any trust in me.

Il n'y a aucun problème, calmez-vous.
There isn't any problem—calm down.

ne ... personne   **no one**

On n'a vu personne hier soir.
We saw no one last night.

Selon Marie, personne ne veut ce boulot.
According to Marie, no one wants this job.

ne...ni...ni...   **neither....nor**

Il n'est ni catholique ni juif, il est musulman.
He's neither Catholic nor Jewish; he's Muslim.

Note that most often the "ne" is dropped in spoken French:

Je veux pas y aller.
I don't want to go there.

Faites pas ça!
Don't do that!